Mastering
Joker Wild
Video Poker

How to Play as an Expert
and
Walk Away a Winner

Bradley Davis

Applied Technology Press
Aurora, Colorado

First printing 1990
Printed in the United States of America
95 94 93 92 91   10 9 8 7 6 5 4 3 2

Library of Congress Catalog Card Number: 90-82847

ISBN 0-9626766-5-9

To Beverly,
my wife and my best friend

Acknowledgments

First and foremost, I would like to thank my wife, Beverly, for her support during this project. Acting as secretary, advisor, editor, breadwinner, and cheerleader, she deserves my greatest appreciation.

Special thanks are also extended to Fred Holborn, Brian Benko, and Kathy Benko for their meticulous review of my manuscript and many helpful comments. Their efforts have resulted in a more readable and better organized book.

I also wish to acknowledge Maryann Guberman for her manuscript review and useful comments, and the wise counsel of Howard Schwartz of Gambler's Book Club and Jim Young of National Writers Club. Jim also did a fine job copyediting this book. Thanks for all of your help and suggestions.

Cover Design by Molly Gough

Table of Contents

Preface

I think you'll love this book! If you already like to play video poker machines that use Jokers, you should very quickly benefit from your purchase. The information contained in these pages should increase your enjoyment, playing skill, and odds of winning. But if you're not familiar with the game, this book is likely to spark your interest. You'll learn that wise machine selection and expert decision-making have much to do with walking away a winner.

Before we get started, however, let me just air a couple of opinions. I personally see little wrong with playing games of skill and chance as a recreational activity. I also know that this view is not shared by everyone. If you feel uneasy about being involved in any form of gambling, then follow your conscience and return this book to the publisher for a full refund.

On the other hand, I do question whether you should play these games as a full-time activity. Even if it's possible to make a living playing certain casino games, I wonder if you should. Does this work benefit society in some way?

My personal belief is that our existence does not end when we die. Our eternal status will depend on our acceptance or rejection of Jesus and the lifestyle that we lived. With this in mind, I would hate to have to justify spending a great deal of time in a casino.

This is a book for the recreational gamer who wants to master the game of Joker Poker. Have fun, play well, but please be sensible.

Introduction

They admit to marathon sessions of 24 hours at a time, pushing those buttons and watching that screen as though hypnotized, waiting for someone to snap their fingers and wake them up. They survive on the questionable nutrition of free drinks and a sandwich or hot dog grabbed and brought back to the machine to eat while they continue playing.
—Dwight and Louise Crevelt, *Slot Machine Mania**

They can't help it! The people described above are hooked! How could something that deals poker hands be so appealing?

Like an invading horde of army ants, these enormously popular machines are gobbling up casino floor space all over the world. Nothing can stop their advance. Even the sacred real estate assigned to craps and blackjack is under constant attack. There has never been anything quite like video poker.

But wait! There are red ants among the black ones! If you look closely, you'll find video poker machines dealing from a *fifty-three* card deck that includes a Joker as a wild card.

---

* Dwight Crevelt and Louise Crevelt, *Slot Machine Mania* (Grand Rapids, Gollehon Press, Inc., 1988), 47.

This new game is called Joker Wild Video Poker, and people have taken to it like bees to honey. Once you start to play these enhanced machines, you quickly get spoiled. Going back to regular video poker is really tough — you'll find yourself aching to see a Joker pop up.

However, having this extra card in your playing deck comes with a price. Joker Poker is a fascinating game set with booby traps. If you don't watch your step, you could easily "blow up" your bankroll.

In regular video poker you occasionally are dealt a difficult hand to play. In Joker Poker these hands are constantly appearing. Remember, the Joker is a wild card that offers many ways to make a winning hand. If you aren't dealt a Joker on the first hand of a new deal, then the more cards you throw away, the greater chance he will appear.

Does that mean marginal hands should always be discarded in hope of capturing the elusive Joker? Or what if you are dealt a Joker? What other cards (if any) should you hold? Very often, the proper way to play is not obvious and wrong choices can be very costly.

Worse yet, payoff charts on certain machines can simply vaporize your playing stake. In regular video poker, most machines have about the same coin return on winning hands. Differences between machines usually are associated with the payoff for a Full House and a Flush. It's easy to spot the best machines.

But not so with Joker Poker! There are at least *nineteen* different versions of payoff charts for this game. Which ones are apt to destroy your bankroll, and which offer a good chance of winning?

This book gives just what you need to maximize your winning potential and playing enjoyment while overcoming all obstacles. Its purpose is to teach you to *master* the game of Joker Wild Video Poker: to play not *like* an expert, but *as* an expert.

Mastering Versus Playing

What's the difference between mastering and playing? Professional tennis tournaments illustrate the distinction.

There are a large number of very good tennis players in the world. However, only a small handful of them can be considered masters of the game. These are the people who consistently do well in the tournaments. Why? Because the truly great players know that winning a match is a lot more involved than serving the ball at 100 miles per hour and having a great backhand.

They know their enemy! Prior to each encounter, the pros choose playing strategies that exploit their opponent's weaknesses. These people have also superbly trained their minds to block out discouragement and distractions. When they play, their performance is at its peak and errors are avoided.

What works well in tennis can also work well for you. In the following chapters you will learn how to select the best machines, properly equip yourself for battle, and then play each hand with deadly accuracy.

The Computer Versus Common Sense

Suppose you were dealt the following hand on a Joker Poker machine:

KC KH 9S 8D 6C*

What would you keep?

Common sense, you might say, would dictate that you should keep the pair of Kings and discard the rest. How right you are; that is always the proper play for this hand.

Now, let's change things just a bit. How would you play this slightly modified hand?

KC KH 9S 8S 6S

Do you keep the Kings or the three cards that could make a Straight Flush?

---

* Throughout this book the letters C, D, H, and S will represent (respectively) the Club, Diamond, Heart, and Spade suits. Using letters for card suits is better than symbols, because card letters are more distinct than card symbols.

Common sense would fail you at this point because sometimes keeping the Kings is best and sometimes it's not *depending on the machine that dealt the hand*. Remember, Joker machines have many varieties of payoff charts. What you hold, and what you throw away, depends on the chart on your particular machine.

No matter what type of Joker Poker machine you are playing, the only way to properly play every hand is with assistance from computer technology. For each machine payoff chart listed in this book, an optimum playing strategy table was developed by an elaborate computer program. Using these strategies, you will never again have to guess which cards to keep and which to throw away. These tables can be taken into casinos, so you don't need a photographic memory to play as an expert.

Incidentally, the playing strategies in this book strike a proper balance between *extreme* accuracy and ease of play. If you have looked ahead to Appendix C or the strategy cards in the back of the book, these listings may already seem a bit long and complicated. However, "complete" tables would be almost ten times larger! The strategies in this book are just the right length. Making the tables longer would never yield more than an additional 0.1% in coin payback.

Trust the strategy tables when deciding how to play your poker hands, but use your common sense to decide how much to invest and how long to play.

Significant Book Features

Detailed Playing Instructions

Part I teaches fundamentals. The mechanics of playing a Joker machine and a review of basic poker hands are topics covered in detail. Also included is a brief example showing how to use this book during an actual playing session and a discussion about common playing pitfalls. Once you have completed this section, you will be able to play Joker Poker and avoid certain errors.

Part II , however, shows you how to master the game. Although most of this section concentrates on selecting the best holdcards by means of the strategy tables and cards, the recommendations concerning playing philosophy and money management also should be of great benefit.

Machine Statistics and Expert Strategy Tables

The tables in Appendix C show you the profit statistics and best way to play any Joker Poker machine you are likely to encounter in the State of Nevada or Atlantic City area. Nineteen different versions of machine payoff charts are analyzed in view of yielding a profit after both long-term and short-term playing sessions. Progressive jackpot machines* are also examined. Following each statistics page, an expert playing strategy is provided.

Short-term winning statistics are a unique book feature. These tables indicate the chances of walking away a winner when you only play brief periods of time.

Expert Strategy Cards

Located at the back of the book are perforated strategy cards that correspond to each of the playing strategy tables in Appendix C. Once you become familiar with the hand classification symbols used on the strategy tables, you may prefer to pull out the strategy cards and use them at the machines of your choice.

---

* Progressive jackpot machines are Joker Poker machines whose best poker hand payoff increases each time a coin is inserted into the machine. Frequently an entire row of machines will be linked to a common progressive money pool. Then, if any machine in that row hits the jackpot hand (usually the Royal Flush), the person playing that machine is awarded the entire amount in the pool. Following the winner's payoff, the jackpot pool is reset to some minimum amount which slowly increases as people continue to play the progressive machines.

Part I

Mastering the Fundamentals

He who would learn to fly one day must first learn to stand and walk and run and climb and dance: one cannot fly into flying.

—Nietzsche, *Thus Spoke Zarathustra*

How to Use This Book

Almost no one will argue about the importance of mastering basics before advanced material. However, it's possible you are already familiar with certain fundamentals such as how to rank poker hands and operate a Joker Poker machine. Your chief interest is how to use the strategy tables and strategy cards.

If this is your situation, you will appreciate that this first chapter is devoted to a brief overview of how to use this book. From my own experience I have found that once I see the "big picture," it's easier to understand and value the details.

A good way to learn something is by an example. Assume you have already read this book at least once and are now ready for some action. The story below describes the use and merit of the various statistics and strategy tables in a typical casino situation.

Suppose you have just walked up to a Joker Poker machine that plays quarters and has the payoff chart shown on the following page.

Final Hand	1 Coin	5 Coins
Royal Flush (natural)	400	4700
Five of a Kind	200	(5 x 200) *
Joker Royal Flush	100	(5 x 100)
Straight Flush	50	(5 x 50)
Four of a Kind	20	(5 x 20)
Full House	7	(5 x 7)
Flush	5	(5 x 5)
Straight	3	(5 x 3)
Three of a Kind	2	(5 x 2)
Two Pair	1	(5 x 1)
Pair of Kings or Better	1	(5 x 1)

Following the instructions described in Chapter 5, "Interpreting the Strategy Tables and Cards," you find that the tables that apply to your machine are on pages 112 and 113. After evaluating the machine statistics on page 112, you determine that this machine has good profit potential. Should you decide to play, you would either use the playing strategy on page 113 or the corresponding strategy card located in the back of the book. (Don't worry about interpreting these tables right now; Chapter 5 will explain everything.)

Before you invest any money, however, you recall from Chapter 8, "Playing Philosophy and Money Management," that just finding a good machine is not enough. To maximize your playing enjoyment and chances of walking away a winner, other things must be considered. For example:

1)   If I had to choose, am I more interested in maximizing long-term or short-term chances for profit? Is this really the

---

* This payoff could have been listed as simply *1000*, but showing it as *(5 x 200)* makes it easy to see that the payoff grows in exact proportion to the number of coins bet. Note that this is not the case for the Royal Flush. Actual machine charts would also indicate payoffs for two, three, and four coins.

best machine for what I'm trying to accomplish right now? Should I consider playing other machines?

2) If I play this machine, what is an appropriate playing stake? How would I feel if I lost my entire investment?

Now, having considered each of the Chapter 8 questions, you set aside a playing stake and decide on a one-hour time limit. After a few other recommended preparation tasks, you finally sit down to play.

Inserting five quarters into the machine, you are dealt the following hand:

```
8C  9C  TD  Joker  KC
```

There are at least four different (but reasonable) ways to play this hand. The best way will be found by classifying each option and then consulting the playing strategy to find the highest (and therefore best) classification.

Using the classification techniques outlined in Chapters 6 and 7, you then categorize the alternatives in your mind and choose candidate holdcards as follows:

Symbol	Definition*	Holdcards
j4CST (O <Qh)	Joker Four-Card Straight, Open-Ended, less than Queen-high	8C 9C TD Joker
jHP	Joker High Pair	Joker KC
j4CFL (1HC)	Joker Four-Card Flush, 1 High Card	8C 9C Joker KC
j3CSF (O)	Joker Three-Card Straight Flush, Open-ended	8C 9C Joker

Now, viewing the column of symbols listed under Joker Hand on your playing strategy (page 113), you note that j4CFL (1HC) is higher in the

---

* Detailed definitions of each symbol are also found in Chapters 6 and 7.

column than any of the other three symbols. The best way to play this
hand, therefore, is to hold everything except the Ten of Diamonds.

You perform a similar procedure on each hand that is dealt during your
playing session. When it is time to quit, you complete a few recommended
departure tasks and then reflect on the events of the past hour. You feel
very good about yourself and your performance and look forward to your
future battles with the machines.

During a playing session, use the playing strategy in Appendix C until
you can classify hands without the help of the Example Hands and the
Symbol Key. When classifying hands becomes easy, you may prefer using
the corresponding strategy card located in the back of this book. The card,
of course, is less cumbersome.

Don't try to memorize the classification order on the tables or cards.
Take this entire book, or just the playing cards, directly to your machine.
Unlike casino table games, you won't have to worry about slowing down
the game while you consult your strategy. Relax, take your time, and
concentrate on playing accuracy.

2

The Mechanics of the Game

The actual procedure for playing Joker Poker machines is simple. In the description that follows, it is assumed you are examining a machine that accepts five coins as a maximum bet. Once you understand the playing mechanics of this device, it will be easy to adapt the procedure to other variations.

Joker Poker machines look a lot like other slot machines except that the game is played on a video display and there's no handle to pull. As you view the playing screen, you will often see five poker cards that were the final result of the last game that was played. The screen usually also indicates whether this previous hand resulted in a win and prompts you to insert a coin.

You begin a new game by inserting coins into the machine. When the first coin is registered, the machine's payoff chart usually pops onto the playing screen and shows the number of coins returned on winning hands. (Some machines, however, have the payoff chart permanently printed above the screen glass.) These payoff amounts then will increase in proportion to the number of coins you put into the machine up to the maximum allowable bet.

The exception to this rule occurs on the highest payoff hand (usually a Royal Flush without a Joker) when the maximum bet is made: the last coin into the machine causes the payoff on the highest hand to jump to the jackpot amount.

If you insert the maximum number of coins, the machine will automatically deal and display a five-card poker hand where each card is selected at random from a fifty-three card deck stored in memory. If you insert less than the maximum number of coins, you must start the game by pressing the DEAL button.

Now the fun begins! After the game is started, five poker cards will appear on the screen. You have only one chance to improve your poker hand. You can keep all of the displayed cards, some of them, or none of them. The cards that you select are called *holdcards* and usually are registered by pressing the HOLD buttons beneath each of the five card positions. If you change your mind at this point, you can retract your decisions by pressing either the HOLD buttons a second time or a separate CANCEL button.

As a final step, you should press the DEAL button again or a separate DRAW button and get new cards for the ones you are throwing away. If you end up with something worth a payoff, money plops down into your payoff tray or credits pile up on your credit meter. If you end up with "garbage" (which happens most of the time), both you and your machine get very quiet.

Speaking of credits, many machines allow your winnings to pile up as credits. You then can play off your credits instead of always having to handle that filthy money.

Personally, I think casinos install credit machines for the same reason that face-up blackjack is frequently offered: more hands per minute means more money per hour *for them*. However, sometimes you can use this credit feature to your advantage. Certain machines will net a long-term profit; more hands per minute means more money per hour *for you*.

When you're playing a credit machine, just be sure to hit the CASH OUT button before you leave. This will convert your hard-earned credits into cold cash.

As a final note, some machines are outfitted with a DOUBLE button that allows you a chance to double your winnings. If you press this button after a win, usually both you and the machine are dealt a card. (Sometimes you can pick your card from four hidden cards.) If the machine's card beats your card, the machine takes your winnings; if your card beats the machine's, your winnings double. If you tie or win, however, you're usually enticed to try again for double or nothing. (I know people who have this same attitude about losing a bet!)

Be aware that when you're using the DOUBLE button, you're really not playing Joker Poker anymore. You're playing roulette and betting on either red or black. Unlike roulette, however, there is no zero or double zero where the house automatically wins. You have an even chance of doubling your money. If you enjoy this feature, that's fine. However, be prepared for larger fluctuations in your playing stake.

Incidentally, don't play the types of double-or-nothing games where the machine always wins if it ties your card or deals itself an Eight. These are poor bets for the player; the house advantages are even greater than playing the American roulette wheel.

3

Who's Who and What Beats What

My wife and I used to play poker with friends almost every month. Before we could begin, however, she always had to find her "what-beats-what" card. (Does a Flush beat a Straight or vice versa and, by the way, what on earth is a Flush?) The purpose of this section is to briefly review the basic types of poker hand classifications and show their order of preference or value. These hands are listed in ascending order of value. If you are a bit rusty at poker games, spending some time in this chapter will make Part II of the book easier to understand.

As a first step, it is necessary to understand the meaning of *rank* and *suit*. Rank refers to the numerical value of a poker card. For example, a Seven of Hearts (7H) and a Seven of Spades (7S) each have the rank of seven. An Ace of Diamonds (AD) has the rank of fourteen, unless it is used in an Ace-low Straight (defined later) or an Ace-low Straight Flush in which case it has a rank of one. A Joker, when dealt in Joker Poker, can assume the rank of any poker card. Another common name for rank is *denomination*.

Suit, on the other hand, refers to the "family name" of a poker card. All poker cards except the Joker belong to one of the following four suits: Clubs, Diamonds, Hearts, Spades. For example, a Two of Hearts (2H) and a Jack of Hearts (JH) are two cards of the same suit. A Joker, when dealt in Joker Poker, can assume the characteristic of any of the four suits.

One Pair

One Pair is defined as two cards of the same rank.

Example: 7C 7D

When playing Joker Poker, it is often necessary to distinguish between a High Pair and a Low Pair. A High Pair has a payoff value; whereas, a Low Pair does not. If you play a Jacks or Better machine, for example, only single pairs with the rank of Jack (11) or above will produce a payoff. A High Pair would be a pair of Jacks, Queens, Kings, or Aces while a Low Pair would be a pair of anything else. When playing a Kings or Better machine, only a pair of Kings or Aces would be considered a High Pair.

Two Pairs

Two Pairs is defined as two cards of one rank plus two cards of a different rank.

Example: 7C 7D QS QH

Three of a Kind

Three of a Kind is defined as three cards of the same rank.

Example: 7C 7D 7S

Straight

A Straight is defined as five cards in rank sequence (no missing cards) but not all of the same suit.

Example: 7C 8D 9S TH JC

In deciding whether a particular poker hand is a Straight, remember that an Ace can be played as either a rank of one or fourteen. If a Straight contains an Ace that is played as a rank of one, the hand is considered an Ace-low Straight; if a Straight contains an Ace played as a rank of fourteen, the hand is considered an Ace-high Straight.

Flush

A Flush is defined as five cards of the same suit but not in rank sequence.

Example: 4C 7C 9C JC QC

Full House

A Full House is defined as two cards of one rank plus three cards of another rank.

Example: 7C 7D QS QH QC

Four of a Kind

Four of a Kind is defined as four cards of the same rank.

Example: 7C 7D 7S 7H

Straight Flush

A Straight Flush is defined as five cards of the same suit that are also in rank sequence.

Example: 7C 8C 9C TC JC

Five of a Kind

Five of a Kind is defined as five cards of the same rank.

Example: 7C 7D 7S 7H Joker

This is the only classification where the Joker is absolutely required. The Joker assumes the same rank as the other four cards. You should also be aware that Five of a Kind is sometimes considered a better hand than a Royal Flush. Many Atlantic City machines, for instance, pay jackpot amounts for Five of a Kind hands instead of Royal Flushes.

Royal Flush

A Royal Flush is a special type of Straight Flush that has a Ten as its lowest ranking card.

Example: TC JC QC KC AC

4

Avoiding Common Pitfalls

If you play Joker Poker for extended periods of time, occasionally you will make some strategy errors even if you use this book. When your mind is fatigued, for example, it's not uncommon to see one pair of cards but completely miss a second pair. The solution to *this* problem is obvious: if you find yourself staring at your display screen for five minutes before you can decide what you've got, take a break.

There is another class of errors, however, more mechanical in nature. The purpose of this chapter is to identify three common errors of this type to help you avoid them.

Changing Horses in Mid-Stream

If you read other books on video poker, you're likely to find helpful advice such as, If you're playing a credit machine, be sure to cash out your credits before you leave. (Even my book advises this.) I must confess, however, that in my heart of hearts, I used to doubt that people would ever forget they have money in a machine. But one day I actually saw this happen.

I was waiting in line to eat at a restaurant in downtown Las Vegas when a woman in front of me decided to play some video poker. Her friends held her place in line as she sat down to play one of the credit machines near the entrance. After a period of time when she had built up a few credits, she decided to play cash instead of working off her credits. Her payoff tray accumulated a few coins as she played.

Suddenly, it was time to eat! Her friends were at the front of the line and were ready to be seated. In a rush she finished her hand, scooped up her money from the payoff tray, and raced by me. She had completely forgotten that she had credits in the machine. (We later found her in the restaurant and gave the money to her.)

By "changing horses in mid-stream" this woman set herself up to forget about her credits. The moral is:

> *If you play with credits, stick to playing credits;*
> *if you play with cash, then stick to playing cash.*

Playing Too Fast

As you become more comfortable playing Joker Poker, you'll find yourself playing faster and faster. The ability to play rapidly is a great asset in video poker tournaments and on Joker Poker machines that give you a long-term profit, but it's also fraught with danger. If you try to play too fast, you're apt to suffer certain consequences.

Let me relate an unfortunate incident. In February 1989 I was playing a Joker Poker machine that gave me about a 1% long-term advantage. My goal was to play the game as fast as I could in order to maximize my per hour profit. I found that by playing a credit machine and using two hands to press the HOLD and DEAL buttons, I could rip through about nine hands per minute. Wow, I felt like Commander Data on Star Trek! My eyes, brain, and hands worked together in perfect harmony. I saw myself as a flawlessly performing robot.*

Then the unspeakable occurred. A new deal popped up Four of a Kind. Hot dog, I said to myself, come on Joker, let's see Five of a Kind! I quickly pressed two HOLD buttons with my left hand, two with my right, and

---

* Technically speaking, however, Commander Data is an *android*, not a robot.

smashed the DEAL button. To my shock and horror, two cards were discarded instead of one. Not only did I not get the Joker that I wanted, but my pat Four of a Kind was reduced to Three of a Kind! Instead of a $100 win, I got back only $10.

My error was mechanical although completely avoidable. On the particular machine I was playing, lingering on one HOLD button while another HOLD button is pushed will cancel the effect of the previous HOLD button. Apparently, after I pressed the second HOLD button with my left hand, my finger remained on this second button as I pressed another HOLD button with my right hand. Only three of the four cards were registered as holdcards when I hit the DEAL button.

From now until the end of time, I'll be thinking about how I could have used that $90 I threw away. Maybe you can benefit from my error. By the way, following this occurrence, I decided never to play Joker Poker using more than one hand.

Other reasons for playing rapidly have their roots in mythology. Let me comment about a few bits of video poker lore that are utter nonsense and bound to give you a lot of grief. To start with, a popular theory is that if you hit those HOLD buttons really fast, you'll "confuse" the machine and it will give you better cards. The people that profess this belief have no idea how rapidly electricity can move. Once you press a HOLD button your decision is registered electronically by the machine. Electrons travel at almost the speed of light. This fact should give nimble fingers a real challenge! More likely than not, playing this way will result in missing (or canceling) a card that you intended to hold.

Another variation of this "I can play faster than you" theme can be even more devastating. Back in Chapter 2, I mentioned that when the maximum number of coins is inserted into most Joker Poker machines, your hand is automatically dealt to you. Somehow, a few people got the notion that it was a good idea to hit the DEAL button before the machine could respond to a maximum-coin bet.

Perhaps they thought that this would trick the machine into giving better cards or that, at least, the machine play would be faster. Normally this doesn't make any difference, except that occasionally one of their coins will fall into the payoff tray because it wasn't accepted and they end up with a four-coin bet instead of their usual five-coin bet.

To give you an idea of what could happen if you follow this misguided theory, I'll summarize a story told by Stanford Wong in his book *Professional Video Poker.*[*] Wong was playing a quarter video poker machine with a progressive Royal Flush jackpot of over $5,000 when the woman next to him hit the elusive Royal. Instead of jumping for glee, however, she was groaning. Her Royal Flush was on four quarters instead of five. Although she had intended to play five coins on every play, her husband had advised her not to wait for the machine to deal after inserting five coins but to press the DEAL button manually. The quarter that failed to register cost the lady over $4,000!

Refusing to Touch a Perfect Poker Hand

About the only positive thing I can say about this last pitfall is that it does my heart good to observe I'm not the only one who makes this silly mistake. The twisted way my mind works at times is not really so uncommon.

The following true story demonstrates the error. After playing video poker for many hours, I was dealt a pat Straight. In my mind I said to myself, At last! I'm dealt a hand that doesn't require any decisions on my part. Everything is perfect; I don't need to touch a thing.

At this point I reached over to the DEAL button expecting the machine to look at my perfect hand and credit me $35 for a Straight. Instead, to my great dismay, every one of my cards was discarded and replaced with five new cards! I had overlooked punching the five HOLD buttons that corresponded to each card of my Straight.

The fact that you need to punch HOLD buttons when you want to improve your hand *does not mean* you don't have to punch HOLD buttons when you don't want to improve your hand. Learn from my error and avoid unhappiness.

---

[*] Stanford Wong, *Professional Video Poker* (La Jolla, Pi Yee Press, 1988), 7.

Part II

Mastering the Discipline

Do not consider painful what is good for you.

—Euripides, *Medea*

5

Interpreting the Strategy Tables
and Cards

Now is the time to examine each part of a typical set of machine strategy tables located in Appendix C. The Two Pair or Better, 20-8-7-6 Machine tables on pages 90 and 91 will be used in all examples. Following the Appendix C discussion, we will finish this chapter by taking a brief look at strategy card features and considerations.

Interpreting the Strategy Tables

Take your time when studying this material. Your decision to play a particular machine will be directly related to your understanding of its strategy tables.

These tables are called strategy tables instead of statistics tables because:

1) An expert playing strategy is included as one of the tables, and;

2) The information presented on these tables will help form your strategy against the machine.

For example, based on statistics from the tables, your strategy may be to play a particular machine only when the payoff for a Royal Flush reaches $4,000.

To make things simple, it will be assumed that all machines require five coins for the maximum bet (the most common variety). Modifications to accommodate three-coin and ten-coin versions can be found in Appendix B.

Title

```
        JOKER WILD TWO PAIR OR BETTER TABLES
                 20-8-7-6 MACHINE
```

Joker machines, strategy tables, and strategy cards are all organized according to their *type* and *sequence*. When you walk up to a Joker machine, check its payoff chart for the lowest winning poker hand. That is your machine's type.

Next, check your machine's one-coin payoffs from Four of a Kind down to a Straight. The value and order of these numbers is your machine's sequence.

To find the information that applies to your machine, turn to the table of contents and find the page numbers for the strategy tables of the same type and sequence, or flip to the back of the book and pull out the strategy card with matching type and sequence. It's that easy!

For example, the title above indicates that these are the tables that should be used for a Joker machine that requires at least Two Pair to win (or break even) and has its one-coin payoffs from Four of a Kind down to a Straight listed (in order) as 20,8,7,6.

Payoff Table

Final Hand	1 Coin	5 Coins
Royal Flush	500	5000
Five of a Kind	100	(5 X 100)
Straight Flush*	50	(5 X 50)
Four of a Kind	20	(5 X 20)
Full House	8	(5 X 8)
Flush	7	(5 X 7)
Straight	6	(5 X 6)
Three of a Kind	2	(5 X 2)
Two Pair	1	(5 X 1)

* Joker Royal Flush counts as Straight Flush.

Notice that only two columns of coin payoffs appear in the table. This was done only to conserve space. The number of coins returned to you on a winning hand will always be the one-coin payoff times the number of coins actually bet. The only exception to this rule applies to the highest payoff hand on the table (the Royal Flush in this case): when the maximum number of coins are bet, the payoff jumps to the jackpot amount (5000 coins).

The one-coin payoffs in the above table should match any Two Pair or Better, 20-8-7-6 Joker machines that you might find. Does this statement make sense to you? After all, only the payoffs from Four of a Kind down to a Straight were actually matched. How do we know that this payoff table agrees with your machine's payoff chart for other hands such as Three of a Kind or a Straight Flush?

The reason everything matches seems to be that, once a Joker machine manufacturer picks a particular sequence of payoffs for Four of a Kind down to a Straight, he always picks the same payoffs for the other winning hands. For instance, I have found that the one-coin payoff for Three of a Kind is two coins on all Two Pair or Better, 20-8-7-6 machines.

Now, having said all this, it is still a good idea to check for perfect matching. Make sure that each of the one-coin payoffs on your machines's payoff chart agrees with the payoff table on its matching strategy tables or card. If there is a disagreement, then the statistics and playing strategy will not be exactly right for your machine and should not be used.

Finally, don't be concerned that the jackpot (highest payoff) amount on your machine's payoff chart is a bit different from the amount shown under 5-Coins on your payoff table. If, for example your machine pays 4000 coins for a five-coin Royal Flush instead of 5000, the playing strategy will remain sufficiently accurate to accommodate this jackpot variation. The five-coin jackpot amount shown in the payoff table is simply the most common amount for that particular machine version.

Long-Term Machine Payback

Fixed Royal Flush Payoff	Machine Payback
5000 (5 Coins)	102.0 %
4700 (5 Coins)	101.9 %
4000 (5 Coins)	101.6 %
500 (1 Coin)	101.0 %

Minimum Progressive Royal Flush
Jackpot Needed for 100% Machine Payback

$	5.95 (5 Nickels)
	29.73 (5 Quarters)
	118.93 (5 Dollars)

Minimum Progressive Royal Flush
Jackpot Needed for 101% Machine Payback

$	129.46 (5 Nickels)
	647.30 (5 Quarters)
	2,589.20 (5 Dollars)

Before examining each of these tables, it is important to understand the meaning of *long-term*. This phrase refers to the average number of hands required to win the highest paying hand on your machine's payoff chart (usually the Royal Flush). The key word in this definition is *average*. Although drawing to a Royal Flush (with no Joker) usually occurs about once every 40,000 hands, you could get one within the first 1000 hands or you may play 100,000 hands and still never hit pay dirt.

When a machine's long-term payback is 100%, you should expect the losses and profits of your individual playing sessions on that machine to approximately balance after an enormous number of poker hands are dealt (like about 40,000 hands on the average). In other words, it will eventually be an even game. When the payback is 101%, you should realize approximately a 1% profit on total money invested. At 99%, you should realize approximately a 1% loss, etc.

Now let's look at the first table. Note that this table applies to machines with a fixed payoff for the jackpot hand (usually the Royal Flush with a five-coin bet). Most Joker machines are of this variety. The number of coins returned on its highest payoff hand will always be the same. Different machines, however, will offer different fixed jackpot amounts, such as 5000, 4700, and 4000 coins. As shown in the right column, machines with these particular fixed payoffs will yield (in order) long-term paybacks of 102%, 101.9%, and 101.6%.

Note that the payback for a one-coin Royal Flush is also listed. If you play less than five coins per bet, this is the payback that you can expect on the total amount of money invested.

Take another look at this table. Now that you have some idea what the numbers mean, do you find this machine at all interesting? You should! This machine returns a long-term profit! The best version can net a 102% payback (2% profit). You'll be hard pressed to find many other casino games that reward expert play so handsomely.

Incidentally, the strategy tables in Appendix C are arranged in descending order of fixed long-term paybacks. Looking back to our example Payoff Table, the most common variety of this 20-8-7-6 machine returns 5000 coins on a Royal Flush when five coins are bet. The number used for ranking this machine within the Two Pair or Better section of Appendix C is the payback associated with this 5000 coin Royal Flush (102%). The strategy cards at the back of the book are arranged in the same manner.

Can you compute long-term profit (or loss*) using this first table? Let's try a few examples.

---

* A loss would be indicated by a computation that results in a negative number.

Example 5-1.

Suppose that you have played about 40,000 hands on a quarter machine that pays 5000 coins on a five-coin Royal Flush (you have really liked this game). Every bet was five quarters. What is your long-term profit?

Answer: $1,000

$$\$0.25 \times 5 \times 40,000 \times 0.020 = \$1,000$$

$$\text{where } 0.020 = (102.0 - 100.0) / 100$$

Example 5-2.

(Same as Example 5-1. except that the machine only pays 4000 coins on a five-coin Royal Flush.)

Answer: $800

$$\$0.25 \times 5 \times 40,000 \times 0.016 = \$800$$

$$\text{where } 0.016 = (101.6 - 100.0) / 100$$

Example 5-3.

Suppose that you have played about 40,000 hands on a dollar machine and every bet was three dollars. What is your long-term profit?

Answer: $1,200

$$\$1.00 \times 3 \times 40,000 \times 0.010 = \$1,200$$

$$\text{where } 0.010 = (101.0 - 100.0) / 100$$

Having completed our discussion of the first table, let's take a look at the last two. These other tables will be of great value when the machine you are considering has a progressive jackpot (see footnote on page 13).

You can know just when your progressive machine yields a long-term profit. In particular, the tables list jackpot amounts needed on nickel, quarter, and dollar machines for 100% and 101% long-term paybacks.

Note that the jackpots are listed in terms of dollars returned instead of coins returned (as in the fixed payback tables). As far as I know, all progressive machines display jackpots in terms of dollar amounts.

You should interpret the information in the second (middle) table as follows:

> When a nickel machine jackpot reaches $5.95, the long-term payback will be *at least*[*] 100% of money invested from that point on, provided that each bet is five nickels.

> When a quarter machine jackpot reaches $29.73, the long-term payback will be at least 100% of money invested from that point on, provided that each bet is five quarters.

> When a dollar machine jackpot reaches $118.93, the long-term payback will be at least 100% of money invested from that point on, provided that each bet is five dollars.

The last table is interpreted in the same manner except that it applies to a 101% payback of money invested.

The advantage of listing both the 100% and 101% amounts is that it makes it very easy to determine your long-term payback when jackpots become even higher. For example, note that the jackpot amounts required for a 100% and 101% payback on a quarter machine are $29.73 and $647.30 respectively. This suggests that for each additional 1% payback, the jackpot amount must increase by the difference between $29.73 and $647.30, namely, $617.57. Using this technique, try to verify that a 103% payback would require a $1,882.44 jackpot on a quarter machine.

---

[*] After each bet is registered, the jackpot amount and the corresponding payback percentage increase slightly. As the machine is played, its payback percentage creeps upward like a bank savings account that earns interest daily.

Finding jackpot amounts required for coin denominations other than the nickel, quarter, and dollar is also a very simple task. Just multiply the jackpot amount by the ratio of the value of the coins under consideration. A dime machine, for example, would require jackpots that are twice as big as nickel machines because dimes are twice as valuable as nickels.

Observing that 100% and 101% paybacks on nickel machines require jackpots of $5.95 and $129.46 respectively, the dime machine would require $11.90 and $258.92. Similarly, machines using five-dollar tokens would require jackpots five times as big as dollar machines or $594.65 and $12,946 respectively.

Short-Term Win/Lose Odds

Odds of Winning	Odds of Losing
45 %	55 %

As a recreational gamer you may be much more interested in your short-term winning potential than your long-term profits. If this is your gaming attitude you will be particularly interested in this section.

The phrase *short-term* is defined as playing 100 hands of Joker Poker. The percentage of times you will walk away either winning or breaking even is shown under Odds of Winning while the percentage of times you will lose is shown under Odds of Losing. This data was derived from 10,000 computer-generated playing sessions of 100 hands each. Results are accurate to within plus or minus 1%.

Short-term winning odds and long-term machine payback are completely different concepts. If you play Joker Poker for just a short period of time and want the very best chance of walking away a winner, try to find a machine whose winning odds are close to 50%. Winning odds of 50% indicate that you have an even chance of breaking even or winning.

On the other hand, if you are more interested in long-term profits, try to find a machine whose long-term payback is greater than 100% of money invested. As discussed earlier, a 100% payback implies that playing session wins and losses will eventually balance.

The 45% winning odds shown in the example table is an exceptionally high win rate. If your playing sessions always consisted of 100 hands of Joker Poker, nearly half of the time you would either break even or walk away with a profit. (To be more precise, you would win or break even 45 out of 100 sessions on the average.) Without the assistance of a computer, there is little chance that anyone could have guessed such a high result. After all, a player needs Two Pair just to get his bet returned.

But, wait! you exclaim, I never play *exactly* 100 hands of Joker Poker in a playing session. How do I determine my odds of winning if I play only 85 hands or as many as 150 hands?

The answer was found by computer simulation. For machines with short-term winning odds of at least 30%, their published 100-hand odds were still accurate within plus or minus 3% for playing sessions of 70 to 200 hands. For machines with short-term winning odds of less than 30%, their published odds were accurate within plus or minus 5% for this same playing session variation. For most machines, longer playing sessions tended to reduce winning odds.

The machine in this example is also unusual because it possesses excellent statistics for *both* long-term payback and short-term winning odds. (It just doesn't get any better than this; you can enjoy the best of both worlds.) Unfortunately, machines like this are quite rare.

For example, consider the Two Pair or Better, 16-8-5-4 machine that pays 4000 coins on a five-coin Five of a Kind (see pages 96 and 97). You will find this machine in many Atlantic City casinos. If you use the playing strategy in this book, your long-term payback will be 97.1% of the money you invest. Since the house advantage is less than 3%, you might reason that your chances of winning after a short playing session are pretty good.

Nothing could be further from the truth! Your chance of winning or breaking-even after 100 hands of play at this machine is only 25% (see bottom of page 96). On the average, you will lose money in three out of four playing sessions!

You should also be on guard when you play progressive jackpot machines. Their payoffs on maximum-coin Royal Flushes may be so high that they possess excellent long-term paybacks. However, like the 16-8-5-4 machine described above, short-term winning odds are often very poor. If your playing time is limited, consider investing money in a fixed jackpot machine that may lose money in the long run but has a better short-term performance.

As a last comment, be aware that the Short-Term Win/Loss Odds table is accurate for *all* of the Royal Flush jackpots listed under Long-Term Machine Payback. This is because the playing strategy is not changed as the number of coins returned on a jackpot varies. Although the playing strategy for this machine was optimized for a 5000-coin Royal Flush, the strategy changes required to optimize a 4000-coin jackpot, for example, would be too insignificant to warrant the effort.

Playing Strategy and Symbol Key

Playing Strategy

Joker Hand	Example	Regular Hand	Example
j5K	j 9H 9C 9D 9S	RF	AH KH QH JH TH
jRF	j AH KH QH JH	SF	9H 8H 7H 6H 5H
		.	
		.	
		.	
j3CST (I)	j 9H — 7C	2CSF (D)	9H — — 6H
jLP (9-5)	j 9H	3CST (I)	9H 8C — 6D
jLP (J)	j JH	2CSF (Y)	9H — — — 5H
jLP (Q)	j QH	2CST (O)	9H 8C
		Draw Five	QH 9C 6D 4S 2H

(2P 20-8-7-6)

- -

Symbol Key

j : Joker	O : Open-ended
RF : Royal Flush	I : Inside
SF : Straight Flush	D : Double-Inside
FH : Full House	Y : Triple-Inside
FL : Flush	
ST : Straight	
2P : Two Pair	
LP : Low Pair (Usually A-2, Aces to Twos)	
MC : Middle Card	

5K,4K,etc. : 5 of a Kind, 4 of a Kind, etc.
4C,3C,etc. : 4-Card, 3-Card, etc.
Ah,Kh,etc. : Ace-high, King-high, etc.

Example

j4CST (D) : Joker 4-Card Straight, Double-Inside

Our discussion of these (abridged) tables will be limited to a brief overview of its content and organization. The meaning of the classification symbols will be thoroughly investigated in Chapter 5, "Classifying Non-Joker Hands" and Chapter 6, "Classifying Joker Hands."

The first column of the Playing Strategy table is concerned with how to determine proper holdcards if you are dealt a hand containing a Joker. Every Joker hand will fall into one or more classifications that appear in this first column. Your job is identify holdcards that fit these various classifications, select the highest classification, and then keep the corresponding holdcards.

The examples in the second column will help you remember the meaning of the classification symbols in the first column. Only holdcards are shown although actual hands would, of course, contain five playing cards. The dashes will help you relate missing cards in potential Straight Flush and Straight hands to their symbolic representations. Looking at the fourth entry from the bottom, for example, the dash between the 9H and 7C would correspond to the *I* (Inside) symbol character in the j3CST (I) classification.

The third and fourth columns are similar to the first two, except that they apply to hands dealt without a Joker. During an actual playing session, you will be using these last two columns about 90% of the time.

The Symbol Key that accompanies the Playing Strategy should be easy to interpret. Note, however, that the symbol for Triple-Inside is the capital letter *Y* and not the capital letter *T*. The T has been reserved as a symbol for cards with the rank of Ten.

Interpreting the Strategy Cards

The strategy cards located in the back of the book are just abbreviated versions of the strategy tables in Appendix C. One side contains a symbolic representation of the Payoff Table while the other lists a shortened version of the Playing Strategy. As mentioned before, you may find these cards more convenient than the tables. The cards are easily carried in a pocket or purse.

Another advantage of the cards over the tables is the addition of color codes to highlight the different *classifications* of poker hands. These poker hands are shown symbolically on the playing strategy side of the card. The color key is as follows:

Classification of Poker Hand	Color Code
Royal Flush	Red
Straight Flush	Yellow
Flush	Blue
Straight	Green

These codes also apply to partial poker hands that could become winning hands when discards are replaced with new cards. For example, a Four Cards to a Flush classification (4CFL) is colored blue because blue is the color of a Flush (FL) classification.

Not only will the different colors help you quickly find desired hand classifications, but they also should aid in avoiding mistakes. For example, the symbols 3CSF (O) and 3CST (O) (which are defined in the next chapter) differ by only one letter. Without the color coding you could easily confuse the two. However, knowing that all potential Straight Flush hands are color-coded in yellow and all potential Straight hands in green, you are less likely to make an error.

Color codes are also used to help distinguish different *types* of Joker machines. This coding will make it easier to find the appropriate card when searching through a stack of them. The following key applies to the payoff table side of all strategy cards:

Type of Joker Machine	Color Code
Two Pair or Better	Red
Kings or Better	Blue
Jacks or Better	Green
Aces or Better	Yellow

During a playing session, I usually place my strategy card just behind the coin slot for easy reference. However, one drawback to this location is that sometimes too much light from the display screen shines through the card making it difficult to distinguish the color codes. If you have the same problem, I suggest that you place additional cards behind your playing card in order to block out more light.

6

Classifying Non-Joker Hands

This chapter and the next will equip you with the tools for expert holdcard selection. In particular, you will learn and practice how to:

1) Identify groups of holdcards that can be represented by poker hand classification symbols, and then;

2) Choose the best group of holdcards based on which classification symbol is ranked highest on the playing strategy table or card.

Within each family of poker hands discussed in this chapter, typical classification symbols are listed and defined along with an example group of holdcards (look ahead to table listed under Pair Family). To best study this material, first learn the meaning of each symbol and then convince yourself that the corresponding holdcards are, indeed, a combination of cards represented by that symbol.

Next, work the problem in reverse. Place your hand over the symbol and definition columns and pick an example group of holdcards from the last column. In your mind determine what symbol classification would apply and then check your answer. Do this a sufficient number of times to prove to yourself that you have mastered classifications for that family of poker hands. When you're through practicing, move on to the next poker hand family and repeat the entire process.

When you have finished studying all families of poker hands, you should be able to look at any combination of five playing cards (without a Joker) and pick groups of holdcards* that correspond to one or more hand classifications. At this point, the only task remaining is to choose the best group of holdcards.

The last job is the easiest of all. Simply select the group of holdcards that correspond to the hand classification that is highest on your strategy table or strategy card.

This chapter ends with a classification drill that will give you practice and build your confidence in correctly applying the playing strategies. Consider working this drill before moving on to the next chapter.

The symbols defined in this chapter appear under Regular Hand on the playing strategy tables and cards. Regular poker hands are hands that don't have a Joker.

Before we begin our detailed study of poker family hand classifications, let's examine two technical issues that could cause some confusion. In Chapter 3, Straights, Flushes, Straight Flushes, and Royal Flushes were all defined as poker hands that involved five cards. However, you will find many hands in this chapter classified as Three-Card Royal Flushes, Four-Card Straights, etc.

I've done this to avoid being too "wordy." These hands could have been classified as Three Cards to a Royal Flush, Four Cards to a Straight, etc., but I think you will prefer the abbreviated definitions. (Recall that in the last chapter, 4CFL was identified as Four Cards to a Flush.)

Similarly, references to members of a poker hand family are sometimes shortened to just the family name. Different types of Three-Card Royal Flush classifications, for example, might simply be called the Royal Flush classifications or the Royal Flush hands. Hopefully, you will always understand the correct intention.

---

* The only exception is a poker hand classified as *Draw Five*. A hand of this classification is considered completely worthless and no holdcards are chosen. (All five cards are discarded.)

Pair Family

Pair Family Classifications		
Symbol	**Definition**	**Example**
4K	Four of a Kind	9H 9C 9D 9S
FH	Full House	9H 9C 8D 8S 8H
3K	Three of a Kind	9H 9C 9D
2P	Two Pair	9H 9C 8D 8S
HP	High Pair	AH AC
LP	Low Pair	9H 9C

Whether or not a pair of cards should be considered a High Pair or a Low Pair depends on the payoff chart of the machine you are playing. As discussed in Chapter 3, a High Pair is a pair of cards that has a payoff value; a Low Pair doesn't. For example, on a Kings or Better Joker Poker machine, only pairs of Kings and Aces are High Pairs. On a Two Pair or Better machine, all pairs are considered Low Pairs.

Flushes

Flush Classifications		
Symbol	**Definition**	**Example**
FL	Flush	9H 7H 5H 3H 2H
4CFL	Four-Card Flush	9H 7H 5H 3H
3CFL	Three-Card Flush	9H 5H 2H

Think of Flush classifications as consolation prizes. When you can't arrange your hand into some type of Straight Flush, call it some type of Flush. Reason like this: Too bad, I tried to make a Four-Card Straight Flush from this hand but the spread was too great; at least I have a Four-Card Flush.

Straight Flushes and Straights

Now things become more interesting. One of the most challenging tasks in mastering Joker Poker is to correctly classify potential Straight Flushes and Straights. The reason that these two types are described together is because Straights can always be thought of as degraded forms of Straight Flushes. (Recall that a Straight hand doesn't have all of its cards in the same suit like a Straight Flush hand.) Everything discussed about classifications for Straight Flushes also applies to Straights.

This section will also introduce qualifier symbols. These are letters and/or numbers found inside parentheses on the playing strategies. The purpose of these symbols is to further qualify the classes of poker hands. As a general rule, the more precisely poker hands are classified, the better the selection of holdcards and the higher the machine payback and odds of winning.

For example, consider the following two hands:

Symbol	Definition	Example
3CSF (O)	Three-Card Straight Flush, Open-ended	9H 8H 7H
3CSF (I)	Three-Card Straight Flush, Inside	9H 8H — 6H

Both of these are Three-Card Straight Flushes but the O stands for Open-ended and has no missing cards or *holes* among its holdcards while the I stands for Inside and has one hole. Even though these hands are very similar, the open-ended version has a better chance for a payoff. On playing strategies you'll always find 3CSF (O) ranked above 3CSF (I).

The most common qualifier symbols for Straight Flush and Straight hands are as follows:

Qualifier Symbol	Definition	Number of Holes
O	Open-ended	0
I	Inside	1
D	Double-Inside	2
Y	Triple-Inside	3

Hands are degraded from O to Y as more holes are found between the highest and lowest holdcards. As mentioned earlier, the letter Y is used for Triple-Inside instead of T. Just think of the letter Y as a symbol that shows three lines intersecting at the center of the letter. This will help you remember that it represents "tripleness."

Typical Straight Flush classifications (with qualifiers) are as follows:

Straight Flush Classifications

Symbol	Definition	Example
SF	Straight Flush	9H 8H 7H 6H 5H
4CSF (O)	Four-Card Straight Flush, Open-ended	9H 8H 7H 6H
4CSF (I)	Four-Card Straight Flush, Inside	9H 8H — 6H 5H
3CSF (O)	Three-Card Straight Flush, Open-ended	9H 8H 7H
3CSF (I)	Three-Card Straight Flush, Inside	9H 8H — 6H
3CSF (D)	Three-Card Straight Flush, Double-Inside	9H 8H — — 5H
2CSF (O)	Two-Card Straight Flush, Open-ended	9H 8H
2CSF (I)	Two-Card Straight Flush, Inside	9H — 7H
2CSF (D)	Two-Card Straight Flush, Double-Inside	9H — — 6H
2CSF (Y)	Two-Card Straight Flush, Triple-Inside	9H — — — 5H
1MC (9-5)	One Middle Card, 9 to 5 (One-Card Straight Flush)	9H

To generate a similar table of Straight classifications, use this Straight Flush list but change all *SFs* to *STs*, all occurrences of *Straight Flush* to

Straight, and change at least one of the cards in each holdcard example to a different suit.

In the holdcard examples above, the holes were always shown next to one another. However, this is not a requirement. Within a sequence of cards, the **number** of holes is important, not their position. For example, a 3CSF (D) could look like this:

$$9H \ — \ 7H \ — \ 5H$$

The last classification on this list, 1MC (9-5), requires a bit of explanation. 1MC stands for One Middle Card and when attached to the qualifier 9-5 means that you are to choose a middle card as a holdcard that is in the range of 9 to 5. It would also be best if the chosen holdcard is "isolated" or furthest from nearby cards.

For example, suppose you were to apply the 1MC (9-5) classification to the following hand:

$$9H \ \ 8D \ \ AC \ \ 5S \ \ 2H$$

Your choice should be the 5S because it is the middle card in the range of 9 to 5 that is most isolated from the other cards. (The 9H is "next to" the 8D, so both of these cards are poorly isolated.) When you keep only one holdcard, there is almost always a chance that your final hand could become a Straight or even a Straight Flush. Choosing a holdcard that is furthest from its neighbors increases your chances of getting those winning hands.

Now that you can appreciate the value of qualifiers, it may surprise you that they're not always used. On some strategy tables, for example, you'll find Four-Card Straight Flushes classified with qualifiers as follows:

$$4CSF \ (O)$$

$$4CSF \ (I)$$

On other tables you will only see the unqualified classification:

$$4CSF$$

Don't be alarmed. This is not an oversight.

Concerning this last case, frequently it doesn't make any difference in your playing strategy if a Four-Card Straight Flush is of the open-ended or inside variety. They both may be of higher playing rank than any of the classifications below them. Why use two lines on a strategy table when a one-line unqualified classification will do just fine?

Before leaving the topic of O to Y qualifiers, we need to look at a few hands that require special treatment. Specifically, some Straight Flush and Straight hands have "stunted growth" and need to have their O to Y symbols degraded somewhat. For example, how would you finish qualifying this hand which has cards at the high end of the deck?

        4CST (?)   AH KC QD JS

Your inclination probably would be to insert an O (Open-ended) because there are no holes between the AH and JH. However, the hand is not open on the ace end. Beginning with the JS, the lowest card, the hand would "like to grow" to one card above the ace but can't. The O qualifier would be wrong.

Fortunately, there is an easy way to find the right qualifier. First, let's look at some procedures and then a few examples (which include the problem above):

Procedure for Qualifying SF and ST Hands at High End of Deck

1) Qualify your hand as you normally would (O for no holes, I for one hole, etc.).

2) Counting *up* from your *lowest* holdcard, determine if the next four highest cards in sequence exist in the playing deck. If they do, no qualifier degrading is required.

3) If all four cards do not exist, perform the subtraction

        4 - (number of cards that do exist) = x

    and then degrade your hand qualifier by "x" levels.[*]

---

[*] Refer back to page 53 for order of levels from O (highest) to Y (lowest).

Procedure for Qualifying SF and ST Hands at Low End of Deck

1) Qualify your hand as you normally would (O for no holes, I for one hole, etc.).

2) Counting *down* from your *highest* holdcard, determine if the next four lowest cards in sequence exist in the playing deck. If they do, no qualifier degrading is required.

3) If all four cards do not exist, perform the subtraction

$$4 - (\text{number of cards that do exist}) = x$$

and then degrade your hand qualifier by "x" levels.

Example 6-1.

Problem: 4CST (?)   AH KC QD JS

Solution: 4CST (I)

How to Solve the Problem:

a) Perform step 1) of High End Procedure and make ? = O (Open-ended).

b) Perform step 2) and recognize that the qualifier must be degraded since only three cards exist above the JS (Queen,King,Ace).

c) Perform step 3). Your subtraction should be

$$4 - 3 = 1$$

and the O qualifier should be degraded one level to I.

Example 6-2.

Problem: 2CSF (?)   3H 2H

Solution: 2CSF (D)

How to Solve the Problem:

a)   Perform step 1) of Low End Procedure and make ? = O (Open-ended).

b)   Perform step 2) and recognize that the qualifier must be degraded since only two cards exist below the 3H (Two,Ace).

c)   Perform step 3). Your subtraction should be

$$4 - 2 = 2$$

and the O qualifier should be degraded two levels to D.

Example 6-3.

Problem: 2CSF (?)   4C — — AC

Solution: 2CSF (Y)

How to Solve the Problem:

a)   Perform step 1) of Low End Procedure and make ? = D (Double-Inside).

b)   Perform step 2) and recognize that the qualifier must be degraded since only three cards exist below the 4C (Three,Two,Ace).

c)   Perform step 3). Your subtraction should be

$$4 - 3 = 1$$

and the D qualifier should be degraded one level to Y.

One last type of qualifier should be examined. Sometimes it is useful to specify whether or not a Straight Flush or Straight hand contains any High Cards. Classifications that contain High Card qualifiers are usually worth more than hands that don't have any. An example of a hand containing one High Card on a Kings or Better machine is as follows:

3CSF (D 1HC)   KH TH 9H

On other machines, multiple High Cards may be present. The High Card symbol, HC, may then be preceded by an asterisk indicating the presence of one or more High Cards. An example of such a hand on a Jacks or Better machine is as follows:

3CSF (I *HC)   QH JH 9H

Royal Flushes

You may wonder why a separate section should be devoted to Royal Flush classifications because, after all, a Royal Flush is really just a special case of a Straight Flush. A Straight Flush whose lowest card is a Ten is (by definition) a Royal Flush.

The reason for making this distinction is that different symbol qualifiers are used. Since Royal Flush hands use cards near the top end of the deck, they are almost always growth stunted. The special High End Procedure discussed in the last section would be in constant use. This would be very tedious.

There is, however, a better way. Royal Flush hands can be qualified by the rank of their highest card. For example, consider qualifying the following hand:

3CRF (?)   KS QS TS

There is no need to count holes between the KS and TS and then apply the High End Procedure. You can qualify the hand by simply noting that the highest card is KS and then inserting the symbol Kh for King-high:

3CRF (Kh)   KS QS TS

Typical Royal Flush classifications (with qualifiers) are as follows:

Royal Flush Classifications

Symbol	Definition	Example
RF	Royal Flush	AH KH QH JH TH
4CRF (Kh)	Four-Card Royal Flush, King-high	KH QH JH TH
4CRF (Ah)	Four-Card Royal Flush, Ace-high	AH — QH JH TH
3CRF (Qh)	Three-Card Royal Flush, Queen-high	QH JH TH
3CRF (Kh)	Three-Card Royal Flush, King-high	KH — JH TH
3CRF (Ah)	Three-Card Royal Flush, Ace-high	AH KH QH
2CRF (Jh)	Two-Card Royal Flush, Jack-high	JH TH
2CRF (Qh)	Two-Card Royal Flush, Queen-high	QH — JH
2CRF (Kh)	Two-Card Royal Flush, King-high	KH — — TH
2CRF (Ah)	Two-Card Royal Flush, Ace-high	AH KH
1CRF (Th)	One-Card Royal Flush, Ten-high	TH
1CRF (Jh)	One-Card Royal Flush, Jack-high	JH
1CRF (Qh)	One-Card Royal Flush, Queen-high	QH
1CRF (Kh)	One-Card Royal Flush, King-high	KH
1CRF (Ah)	One-Card Royal Flush, Ace-high	AH

Referring back to the previous section on Straight Flushes and Straights, recall that sometimes these hands are further qualified by indicating whether or not they contain any High Cards. This can also be true of Royal Flush hands. In addition, the complete absence of any qualifiers is also common. For example, if it makes no difference to your playing strategy that a 4CRF is qualified as Ah or Kh, then the strategy table will simply list the hand classification as a 4CRF.

Classification Drill for Non-Joker Hands

To gain confidence in classifying non-Joker hands and then picking the best group of holdcards, spend some time completing the tables on the following pages. This drill will give you practice playing against the two most popular types of Joker machines in use today: the Two Pair or Better and the Kings or Better.

Complete the first drill table using the Two Pair or Better, 20-8-7-6 playing strategy on page 91. Then, complete the second table (on back side of first table) using the Kings or Better, 20-7-5-3 playing strategy on page 113. *Whenever faced with a situation where there is more than one way to classify a hand, always choose the classification that is highest on the playing strategy that you're using.*

When you look over your completed tables, I think you'll be amazed how often different holdcards were selected depending on which strategy you were using. To find out how you scored, check your answers against the correctly completed tables in Appendix A.

Initial 5-Card Hand	Two Pair or Better 20-8-7-6 Machine	
	Classification	Holdcards
9H AC JC QC AS	3CRF (Ah)	AC QC JC
5H TC 5D 5S 9C		
AH QC 5D TS JH		
9H 8S QD 5S 2H		
5H 8S AH TS 4H		
QH 8H JC 9H TH		
4H 9C 3H 6H 9S		
5D TH QC 9H 3S		
8H 6C 6D 8S 8C		
AH QS JD 4H 9H		
JH TH KC AD 8S		
5H KH KD 4H 5D		
2H QC AH 9D 8S		
3H QD 8H 7C TD		
TH QD QS TD JD		
KH 8C 7D 6S KS		
JH QC TH KS 8H		
TS AS JS KH QS		
7H 6D TS QD 5H		
6H 4D 9C 2D KS		

Initial 5-Card Hand	Kings or Better 20-7-5-3 Machine	
	Classification	Holdcards
9H AC JC QC AS	3CRF	AC QC JC
5H TC 5D 5S 9C		
AH QC 5D TS JH		
9H 8S QD 5S 2H		
5H 8S AH TS 4H		
QH 8H JC 9H TH		
4H 9C 3H 6H 9S		
5D TH QC 9H 3S		
8H 6C 6D 8S 8C		
AH QS JD 4H 9H		
JH TH KC AD 8S		
5H KH KD 4H 5D		
2H QC AH 9D 8S		
3H QD 8H 7C TD		
TH QD QS TD JD		
KH 8C 7D 6S KS		
JH QC TH KS 8H		
TS AS JS KH QS		
7H 6D TS QD 5H		
6H 4D 9C 2D KS		

7

Classifying Joker Hands

I'm always thrilled to see a Joker pop up at the beginning of a new deal. There are so many ways that the hand can end up a winner! Unlike many Friday-night poker games where Jokers can only be used for Aces, Straights, and Flushes, Joker Wild Video Poker has no such restrictions. A Joker can be anything you need to help your hand become a paying hand. You should always enjoy classifying Joker hands.

The last chapter dealt with the definition of the symbols listed under Regular Hand on the playing strategy tables. Now we will concentrate on the other column marked Joker Hand. This column should be consulted only if a Joker is dealt as part of the first five cards of a new deal. On the average, this will occur about once every ten deals.

Much of the material discussed in the previous chapter also applies to this chapter. To avoid repetition, only new information unique to Joker hands will be presented. Note that in all the examples the symbol used for a Joker is the small case letter j.

Before proceeding further, study the following general procedure for classifying Joker hands and the illustrative example hands. This procedure relies heavily on your ability to classify non-Joker hands. Once you determine that each of the example hands is correctly classified, you should progress rapidly through the rest of the chapter.

General Procedure for Classifying Joker Hands [*]

1) Classify your hand as though there was no Joker.

2) Increase the classification rank by one card.

3) Add the symbol j to the beginning of the classification.

Examples

Selected Holdcards	Classification without Joker	Classification with Joker
j 9H 9C 8D 8S	2P	jFH
j 9H 7C	2CST (I)	j3CST (I)
j TH	1CRF (Th)	jLP (T)
j 9H 9C 9D	3K	j4K
j 9H 8H	2CSF (O)	j3CSF (O)
j 9H 6H 3H	3CFL	j4CFL
j 9H 9C	LP	j3K
j 9H 8C 5D	3CST (D)	j4CST (D)
j 9H	1MC (9-5)	jLP (9-5)
j 9H 8H 7H 6H	4CSF (O)	jSF

---

[*] David Gerhardt and Tony Korfman, *Video Poker: Playing to Win* (Las Vegas, Gaming Books International, Inc., 1987), 46. This booklet contains a similar classification method.

Joker Pair Family

Joker Pair Family Classifications		
Symbol	**Definition**	**Example**
j4K	Joker Four of a Kind	j 9H 9C 9D
jFH	Joker Full House	j 9H 9C 8D 8S
j3K	Joker Three of a Kind	j 9H 9C
jHP (A)	Joker High Pair	j AH
jLP (T)	Joker Low Pair	j TH

Qualifier symbols are only used with the Joker Low Pair and Joker High Pair classifications. A complete list is as follows:

Qualifier Symbol	Definition
A	Ace
K	King
Q	Queen
J	Jack
T	Ten
9 - 5	Nine to Five

Probably the only symbol that requires more explanation is the 9-5 qualifier as it is used with Joker Low Pairs. Recall the earlier discussion about the 1MC (9-5) classification. Isolated cards in the middle range of the deck sometimes had a better chance of becoming a winning hand than drawing five new cards.

By similar reasoning, Joker Low Pairs sometimes should be chosen among middle cards (Nine to Five) that are furthest away from their neighbors. Whenever you start with a Joker Low Pair, it's almost always possible that the final hand could become a Joker Straight Flush or Joker Straight.

For example, if you were dealt

j 9H 8C 5D 2S

and knew from your playing strategy that the correct holdcards would be the Joker and a middle card, your best choice would be the Joker and the 5D. The 5D is more isolated than the other middle cards (9H and 8C) and, therefore, has the greatest chance of becoming part of a Joker Straight Flush or Joker Straight.

Before we leave this section, note that Joker Two Pair was not listed among the Joker Pair Family hand classifications. The reason for this is that it's impossible to get Two Pair if you have a Joker as part of your hand![*]

Actually, that's not quite true. It's really a matter of how you want your hand to be considered by the machine. For example, look at the following hand:

j 9H 7C 7D 4S

Wouldn't you really prefer that your machine call this three Sevens (Joker Three of a Kind) rather than a pair of Nines and a pair of Sevens (Joker Two Pair)? Every Joker Two Pair hand is more wisely called a Joker Three of a Kind hand.

Joker Flushes

Joker Flush Classifications		
Symbol	**Definition**	**Example**
jFL	Joker Flush	j 9H 7H 5H 3H
j4CFL	Joker Four-Card Flush	j 9H 6H 3H

As in the previous discussion of Flush hands without a Joker, you should get into the habit of first trying to classify your hand as some type

---

[*] Gerhardt and Korfman, *Video Poker: Playing to Win*, 46 (see footnote on page 64). The impossibility of a Joker Two Pair was expressed in this booklet.

of Joker Straight Flush hand. If the card spread is too great, you can always fall back to classifying your hand as a Joker Flush hand.

Qualifiers are only used with Joker Four-Card Flushes. They indicate if there are any High Cards in the hand. Having a High Card present should always bring a smile to your face; you can't lose in a situation like this. No matter what card replaces your discard, you will at least end up with a Joker High Pair (jHP). An example of such a hand on a King or Better machine is as follows:

j4CFL (1HC)   j AH 9H 6H

Joker Straight Flushes and Straights

The only new item for these families of hand classifications is the addition of the < qualifier. This symbol represents the phrase *less than* and is always used with other qualifiers.

The < qualifier limits the rank of the highest card in a Joker Straight hand classification as in the following example:

j4CST (O <Qh)   j 9H 8C 7D

The holdcards shown on the right form a Joker Four-Card Straight, Open-ended, Nine-high (9h). This hand correctly falls within the range of the qualifiers that specify that it must be less than Queen-high (<Qh).

Probably the greatest hindrance to correct classification is the temptation to first use the Joker to fill in a hole in a Joker Straight Flush or Joker Straight hand and then classify the hand. Don't do this! Follow the general procedure at the beginning of this chapter.

Typical Joker Straight Flush classifications (with qualifiers) are as follows:

Joker Straight Flush Classifications

Symbol	Definition	Example
jSF	Joker Straight Flush	j 9H 8H 7H 6H
j4CSF (O)	Joker Four-Card Straight Flush, Open-ended	j 9H 8H 7H
j4CSF (I)	Joker Four-Card Straight Flush, Inside	j 9H 8H — 6H
j4CSF (D)	Joker Four-Card Straight Flush, Double-Inside	j 9H 8H — — 5H
j3CSF (O)	Joker Three-Card Straight Flush, Open-ended	j 9H 8H
j3CSF (I)	Joker Three-Card Straight Flush, Inside	j 9H — 7H
j3CSF (D)	Joker Three-Card Straight Flush, Double-Inside	j 9H — — 6H
j3CSF (Y)	Joker Three-Card Straight Flush, Triple-Inside	j 9H — — — 5H

A similar list of Joker Straight classifications can be generated by the same techniques used for non-Joker Straights described in the previous chapter.

Joker Royal Flushes

Joker Royal Flush Classifications		
Symbol	**Definition**	**Example**
jRF	Joker Royal Flush	j AH KH QH JH
j4CRF (Qh)	Joker Four-Card Royal Flush, Queen-high	j QH JH TH
j4CRF (Kh)	Joker Four-Card Royal Flush, King-high	j KH QH JH
j4CRF (Ah)	Joker Four-Card Royal Flush, Ace-high	j AH KH QH
j3CRF (Jh)	Joker Three-Card Royal Flush, Jack-high	j JH TH
j3CRF (Qh)	Joker Three-Card Royal Flush, Queen-high	j QH JH
j3CRF (Kh)	Joker Three-Card Royal Flush, King-high	j KH QH
j3CRF (Ah)	Joker Three-Card Royal Flush, Ace-high	j AH KH

Joker Royal Flushes are classified the same way as their non-Joker counterparts except that there are no One-Card or Two-Card Joker Royal Flush hands. (Joker Two-Card Royal Flushes are classified as either Joker Low Pairs (jLP) or Joker High Pairs (jHP).)

Classification Drill for Joker Hands

For the same reasons that you worked the drill for non-Joker hands, spend some time completing the tables on the following pages. As in the previous exercise, complete the first drill table using the Two Pair or Better, 20-8-7-6 playing strategy on page 91 and complete the second table using the Kings or Better, 20-7-5-3 playing strategy on page 113.

As noted in the last drill, *whenever faced with a situation where there is more than one way to classify a hand, always choose the classification that is highest on the playing strategy that you're using.* When finished, check your answers against the correctly completed tables in Appendix A.

Initial 5-Card Hand	Two Pair or Better 20-8-7-6 Machine	
	Classification	Holdcards
j JH 6C QD KS	j4CST (I)	j KS QD JH
j TH 7C QH JH		
j 9H 8C 8D 5S		
j 3H 5C TD 8S		
j AH TC 5H 9S		
j QH TC JH 5S		
j KH 8H 7H 3S		
j 7H 9H 8H 3H		
j 9H KC 6D 3S		
j QH 3D 2C JC		
j 9H 7C 7D 9S		
j 9H 3C 6H AS		
j QH 3C AD KC		
j TH QH 5H AH		
j 5H 7C 8D QS		
j 6H 7C 9H 8H		
j 9H AC 8H QC		
j 6H 2H 3H 6S		
j TH QH 3C 4H		
j 4H 3C 8D QH		

Initial 5-Card Hand	Kings or Better 20-7-5-3 Machine	
	Classification	Holdcards
j JH 6C QD KS	jHP	j KS
j TH 7C QH JH		
j 9H 8C 8D 5S		
j 3H 5C TD 8S		
j AH TC 5H 9S		
j QH TC JH 5S		
j KH 8H 7H 3S		
j 7H 9H 8H 3H		
j 9H KC 6D 3S		
j QH 3D 2C JC		
j 9H 7C 7D 9S		
j 9H 3C 6H AS		
j QH 3C AD KC		
j TH QH 5H AH		
j 5H 7C 8D QS		
j 6H 7C 9H 8H		
j 9H AC 8H QC		
j 6H 2H 3H 6S		
j TH QH 3C 4H		
j 4H 3C 8D QH		

8

Playing Philosophy and Money Management

To master the game of Joker Poker, wisdom must accompany technique. While the previous two chapters focused on how to select the best holdcards, this final chapter develops a playing philosophy that can enhance enjoyment and increase chances for success. Guidelines for proper money management also are discussed. Desired behavior is shown in the fictitious story below, followed by clarification of some important points.

Suppose you and a few friends have just walked into a casino you never visited before. Since everyone in the group likes Joker Poker, you all start down the aisles to find machines to play. From this moment on, however, you begin to do several peculiar things.

Instead of running up to a machine, plunking in a few coins, and beginning to play, you first decide to survey all the different types of Joker Poker machines throughout the building. You note that some games require Two Pair for the lowest payoff while others need only a Pair of Kings. You further observe that among these two different types of machines there are subtle differences in the payoff charts.

For example (and this is most common), the machine in front of you pays 15 for 1 on Four of a Kind but the one right next to it pays 20 for 1 on the same hand. Both machines are the Kings or Better type and there are no other differences between the two machines.

For each Joker machine you find, you match its payoff chart with the appropriate strategy tables in Appendix C. You then evaluate each machine in terms of its playing statistics.

When this initial task is completed, you ask yourself a number of important questions:

1) In view of the survey results, are there Joker Poker games in this casino that I would consider worth playing?

2) Do I really want to play Joker Poker right now?

3) Am I mentally alert?

4) How long do I want to play?

5) How much would I feel comfortable in investing?

6) How would I react if I quickly lost all of the money that I have chosen to invest?

7) At this particular moment, what would be most entertaining to me — to break up my playing investment into small units (like nickels and quarters) and be happy with smaller payoffs but longer periods of play, or large units (like dollars) with larger payoffs but, possibly, shorter periods of play?

8) If I had to pick between the two, would I rather choose to maximize long-term machine payback or my short-term chances of winning?

Having considered each these questions, you decide to play Joker Poker for about an hour since you feel fine and there are a couple of good machines in the casino. With respect to the amount of money you want to invest, your reasoning follows this line of argument:

As of this moment my meals and entertainment have cost me $50. That money was well spent in view of the enjoyment I received. I would be willing to invest (and possibly lose) an equal amount of money playing Joker Poker, but I want the very best chance of walking away a winner when my hour of play is over.

You have found two different types of Joker machines you consider to be good. One is a progressive jackpot machine that requires the maximum bet of five dollars per play in order to qualify for the Royal Flush jackpot. The other machine is a quarter machine with a fixed Royal Flush jackpot.

The matching strategy tables in Appendix C indicate that the current jackpot amount on the progressive machine gives you a 101% long-term payback on your money. The fixed jackpot (quarter) machine, on the other hand, earns a 99% payback with five coins bet per play.

You wisely choose to play the quarter machine for the following reasons:

1) The strategy tables also tell you that the quarter machine yields a 40% short-term chance of winning; whereas, the dollar machine only gives you a 25% chance.

2) The risk of losing $50 on the progressive dollar machine is much greater than the quarter machine. (A $50 playing stake on the dollar machine can be divided only into a few bets.)

Just prior to your gaming session, you find your friends and tell them you are going to invest $50 playing Joker Poker and they shouldn't be surprised if you lose all of it. (The reason for doing this will be discussed at the end of the chapter.) Now you buy $50 in quarters and find a suitable machine. In just a few more minutes you'll be ready to play.

Checking the area around your machine you discover there are no extra slot cups in the vicinity. This prompts you to acquire some from a change booth attendant. You do this to avoid drawing attention to yourself should you happen to hit a big payoff like a Straight Flush. Instead of letting those coins drop into the payoff tray and cause a lot of racket, they can quietly fall into one of your extra cups.

There was a time when you enjoyed the attention and noise whenever you won a few coins. However, that was before you started winning more frequently.

One thing you have learned is that strangers in the seats around you do not *genuinely* rejoice in your good fortune but usually just wish that they were doing as well. Furthermore, some casino personnel may tend to make you feel guilty about your winnings, as if you owed them some of your money. You reason that on really big payoffs like a Royal Flush you would offer a courtesy tip, but you need the smaller payoffs to help balance previous losses. The extra cups help to camouflage a winning session.

Sitting down at your machine, you now make several entries in your gaming log. (This booklet is carried with you whenever visiting casinos.) You record the current date and time, the type of machine you are going to play, and the machine's serial number. This is done because you know that at the end of the year you are required to pay income tax on your winnings. Losses can be deducted from winnings but most people have difficulty proving losses when the IRS is aware of one or more large win. (Currently, the win must be $1,200 or more.) You know that having a gaming log does not guarantee you will be successful in proving losses, but without it you hardly stand a chance.

As the final step in your preparation ritual, you locate the playing strategy table that tells how best to play each hand. You know that this table is listed both in Appendix C and on one of the strategy cards. Since you are quite familiar with the classification symbols, you decide to use the strategy card and place it behind the coin slot of your machine.

During the course of your one-hour playing session you frequently review your strategy card to make sure you don't overlook some valuable holdcard combination. Also, in keeping with your goal to play each hand as well as it possibly can be played, you decide to consume very little (if any) alcohol during that one-hour period.

At the end of the playing session, you open up your gaming log to the appropriate page and enter the current time and the amount won or lost. Then you pick up your strategy card and quietly transfer your winnings from the payoff tray to one of your empty slot cups. (If you were playing a credit machine you would cash out your credits into a slot cup.) When finished, you turn in your money at a change booth.

As you begin your search to find your friends, you reflect on the following truths:

1) I have just played my chosen game in a manner that can truly be classified as expert play. There is most likely no one in this entire casino that could have played my machine better than I have during this past hour.

2) People like me are not paying the casino light bill. If everyone played as skillfully as I just have, casinos would go out of business!

These facts, you remind yourself, are valid regardless of whether the playing session resulted in a win or a loss.

The person described above has mastered the game of Joker Wild Video Poker. He has prepared his mind for peak performance, created a relaxed playing environment, studied his opponent's weaknesses, and then used an optimum playing strategy during his gaming session. *Can you see yourself as this individual?*

It would be helpful now to elaborate on a few important items. The specific areas relate to mental conditioning and money management.

Playing Joker Poker is a lot like "playing the numbers" at the roulette table. Both games are characterized by long periods of losing followed by glorious wins on a big payoff event. If you're only playing your favorite number at roulette, it's easy to become discouraged when spin after spin the croupier takes away your losing bet. Then, just when you're in your deepest depression, your number hits and your playing stake "gets well" again. Since Joker Poker acts the same way, you need to mentally prepare yourself for these sensational excursions and perhaps modify your views on a proper money investment per playing session.

The following incident further illustrates this point. A good friend of mine enjoys playing single-deck blackjack in Las Vegas. He can usually play for hours on a ten or twenty-unit playing stake. One day I set up my computer to automatically play a version of Joker Poker that was among the best fixed jackpot games in the world today. When the space bar on the keyboard was initially tapped, the computer would deal a poker hand and select the best holdcards. A second tap replaced the discards with new cards, evaluated the final result, and displayed total winnings versus total money invested and hands played. Another tap would start the cycle over again.

I asked my friend to tap the space bar and pretend that he was actually playing the game instead of the computer. After about fifty or sixty hands of watching his bankroll steadily erode, he suddenly remarked, "Now is the time that I would really start getting mad!" Shortly after these words left his mouth, he hit a big payoff that almost made him even again. I don't think he'll ever be a real fan of Joker Poker. This sort of thing never happened to him in blackjack, and he just wasn't prepared for his bankroll fluctuations.

Playing Joker Poker can be like riding an emotional roller coaster. When you sit down to play, brace yourself for the valleys and heights you are bound to experience.

So then, knowing that your bankroll can take some big dips, how much money should you invest per playing session? Four questions need to be considered:

1)   What are the game's short-term odds of winning?

2)   How long do I want to play?

3)   How fast do I play?

4)   How much money would I feel comfortable investing and, perhaps, completely losing during the play period?

In the "ideal player" story, $50 was determined to be a comfortable playing stake. When deciding which machine to play, the progressive dollar machine was bypassed in favor of the quarter machine. This was done because the $50 stake could be divided into more playing units and the short-term odds of winning were higher on the quarter machine. At five coins per bet, the dollar machine would have given him only a ten-unit stake; whereas, the quarter machine gave him a forty-unit stake. Ten units was certainly too small but forty units, as shown below, was about right.

The following recommendations are based on playing sessions that could be as low as 70 or as high 200 hands of play:

Short-Term Winning Odds of Desired Game	Recommended Playing Stake
40% and above	40 units
30% to 39%	60 units
29% and below	80 units

These recommendations assume that winnings accumulated in your machine's payoff tray are considered part of your total playing session bankroll. By similar reasoning, credits earned on a credit machine also should be available for machine play during the course of the playing session.

As a final clarification related to the story, I will explain our ideal person's remarks to his friends. Recall that he told them exactly how much he was going to invest. He also said that they shouldn't be surprised if he lost it all during his playing session. This is another aspect of mental conditioning that will help you play better and enjoy the game more. The reasons for his statements are as follows:

1) When a gaming session ends in a loss, few people enjoy admitting it to their friends. So many people relate losing to being a loser. By telling everyone in advance that you plan to risk and probably lose a certain amount of money, you take away much of the sting of losing. You also leave the distinct impression that you are in control of your life and your money.

2) Losing less than you predicted is sort of like winning a second-place award. For example, if you lose only half of the amount you say you're going to invest, you (and everyone else) are much more apt to to think that you really didn't do so badly.

3) Your playing session will be much more relaxed and enjoyable. You no longer feel the pressure of having to show a profit.

4)   Winning, when it happens, will be so much sweeter! When you tell your friends there is a good chance of losing a certain amount of money but then end up winning, they will tend to think you've underestimated yourself: you have a lot more "on the ball" than you realize.

Let me end with some encouragement and a caution. Playing Joker Poker can (and should be) an enjoyable and challenging activity. If you are willing to spend a little time and effort, you can become a master of the game. Depending on the machines you play, it can also be a profitable pastime. I love this game and always enjoy my battle sessions.

On the other hand, if you find yourself becoming obsessed with trying to hit a jackpot or getting back money that you previously lost, you should question whether this is a good way to spend your time. Playing marathon sessions of Joker Poker only because you are extremely bored is another danger sign.

Master the game but don't make a career of it. Life has better things to offer.

Appendix A

Answers to Classification Drills

Answers to Non-Joker Hand Drill

Initial 5-Card Hand	Two Pair or Better 20-8-7-6 Machine	
	Classification	Holdcards
9H AC JC QC AS	3CRF (Ah)	AC QC JC
5H TC 5D 5S 9C	3K	5H 5D 5S
AH QC 5D TS JH	4CST (I)	AH QC JH TS
9H 8S QD 5S 2H	2CST (O)	9H 8S
5H 8S AH TS 4H	3CSF (D)	5H 4H AH
QH 8H JC 9H TH	ST	QH JC TH 9H 8H
4H 9C 3H 6H 9S	3CSF (I)	6H 4H 3H
5D TH QC 9H 3S	2CSF (O)	TH 9H
8H 6C 6D 8S 8C	FH	8H 8S 8C 6C 6D
AH QS JD 4H 9H	3CFL	AH 9H 4H
JH TH KC AD 8S	4CST (I)	AD KC JH TH
5H KH KD 4H 5D	2P	KH KD 5H 5D
2H QC AH 9D 8S	2CSF (Y)	2H AH
3H QD 8H 7C TD	2CRF (Qh)	QD TD
TH QD QS TD JD	3CRF (Qh)	QD JD TD
KH 8C 7D 6S KS	LP	KH KS
JH QC TH KS 8H	4CST (O)	KS QC JH TH
TS AS JS KH QS	4CRF	AS QS JS TS
7H 6D TS QD 5H	3CST (O)	7H 6D 5H
6H 4D 9C 2D KS	2CSF (D)	4D 2D

Initial 5-Card Hand	Kings or Better 20-7-5-3 Machine	
	Classification	Holdcards
9H AC JC QC AS	3CRF	AC QC JC
5H TC 5D 5S 9C	3K	5H 5D 5S
AH QC 5D TS JH	2CRF (Ah 1HC)	AH JH
9H 8S QD 5S 2H	Draw Five	(discard all)
5H 8S AH TS 4H	3CSF (D 1HC)	5H 4H AH
QH 8H JC 9H TH	4CSF	QH TH 9H 8H
4H 9C 3H 6H 9S	LP	9C 9S
5D TH QC 9H 3S	Draw Five	(discard all)
8H 6C 6D 8S 8C	FH	8H 8S 8C 6C 6D
AH QS JD 4H 9H	1CRF (1HC)	AH
JH TH KC AD 8S	2HC	AD KC
5H KH KD 4H 5D	2P	KH KD 5H 5D
2H QC AH 9D 8S	1CRF (1HC)	AH
3H QD 8H 7C TD	2CRF (0HC)	QD TD
TH QD QS TD JD	2P	QD QS TH TD
KH 8C 7D 6S KS	HP	KH KS
JH QC TH KS 8H	4CST (0 Kh)	KS QC JH TH
TS AS JS KH QS	4CRF	AS QS JS TS
7H 6D TS QD 5H	Draw Five	(discard all)
6H 4D 9C 2D KS	1CRF (1HC)	KS

Answers to Joker Hand Drill

Initial 5-Card Hand	Two Pair or Better 20-8-7-6 Machine	
	Classification	Holdcards
j JH 6C QD KS	j4CST (I)	j KS QD JH
j TH 7C QH JH	j4CRF (Qh)	j QH JH TH
j 9H 8C 8D 5S	j3K	j 8C 8D
j 3H 5C TD 8S	jLP (T)	j TD
j AH TC 5H 9S	j3CST (O)	j TC 9S
j QH TC JH 5S	j4CST (O)	j QH JH TC
j KH 8H 7H 3S	j3CSF (O)	j 8H 7H
j 7H 9H 8H 3H	jFL	j 9H 8H 7H 3H
j 9H KC 6D 3S	jLP (9-5)	j 9H or j 7D
j QH 3D 2C JC	j3CST (I)	j QH JC
j 9H 7C 7D 9S	jFH	j 9H 9S 7C 7D
j 9H 3C 6H AS	j3CSF (D)	j 9H 6H
j QH 3C AD KC	j4CST (D)	j AD KC QH
j TH QH 5H AH	jFL	j AH QH TH 5H
j 5H 7C 8D QS	j4CST (I)	j 8D 7C 5H
j 6H 7C 9H 8H	jST	j 9H 8H 7C 6H
j 9H AC 8H QC	j3CSF (O)	j 9H 8H
j 6H 2H 3H 6S	j4CSF (D)	j 6H 3H 2H
j TH QH 3C 4H	j4CFL	j QH TH 4H
j 4H 3C 8D QH	j3CST (I)	j 4H 3C

Initial 5-Card Hand	Kings or Better 20-7-5-3 Machine	
	Classification	Holdcards
j JH 6C QD KS	jHP	j KS
j TH 7C QH JH	j4CRF	j QH JH TH
j 9H 8C 8D 5S	j3K	j 8C 8D
j 3H 5C TD 8S	jLP (T)	j TD
j AH TC 5H 9S	j3CSF (Y 1HC)	j 5H AH
j QH TC JH 5S	j3CRF (Qh)	j QH JH
j KH 8H 7H 3S	j4CFL (1HC)	j KH 8H 7H
j 7H 9H 8H 3H	j4CSF (O)	j 9H 8H 7H
j 9H KC 6D 3S	jHP	j KC
j QH 3D 2C JC	jDraw Four	(discard all)
j 9H 7C 7D 9S	jFH	j 9H 9S 7C 7D
j 9H 3C 6H AS	jHP	j AS
j QH 3C AD KC	jHP	j AD or j KC
j TH QH 5H AH	j4CRF	j AH QH TH
j 5H 7C 8D QS	jLP (9-5)	j 5H
j 6H 7C 9H 8H	j4CSF (I)	j 9H 8H 6H
j 9H AC 8H QC	j3CRF (Ah)	j AC QC
j 6H 2H 3H 6S	j3K	j 6H 6S
j TH QH 3C 4H	j3CRF (Qh)	j QH TH
j 4H 3C 8D QH	jLP (9-5)	j 8D

Appendix **B**

Modifying Tables for Three-Coin and Ten-Coin Machines

Back in Chapter 5, you were told that all strategy tables assume that five coins are required for the maximum bet. Now you will learn how to modify these tables if your particular machine requires three coins or ten coins as the maximum bet.

As in the case of five-coin machines, the first step is to find the strategy tables that match your machine's payoff chart. When this is accomplished, multiply all quantities on these tables that relate to a five-coin bet by 3/5 for a new set of three-coin tables or 10/5 for a new set of ten-coin tables. For example, using the Two Pair or Better, 20-8-7-6 Machine tables on pages 90 and 91, the required changes are shown on the following page.

Payoff Table Changes

Original 5-Coin Tables	Modification to 3-Coin Tables	Modification to 10-Coin Tables
5 Coins	3 Coins	10 Coins
5000	3000	10,000
(5 x 100)	(3 x 100)	(10 x 100)
(5 x 50)	(3 x 50)	(10 x 50)
(5 x 20)	(3 x 20)	(10 x 20)
(5 x 8)	(3 x 8)	(10 x 8)
(5 x 7)	(3 x 7)	(10 x 7)
(5 x 6)	(3 x 6)	(10 x 6)
(5 x 2)	(3 x 2)	(10 x 2)
(5 x 1)	(3 x 1)	(10 x 1)

Long-Term Machine Payback Changes

Original 5-Coin Tables	Modification to 3-Coin Tables	Modification to 10-Coin Tables
5000 (5 Coins)	3000 (3 Coins)	10,000 (10 Coins)
4700 (5 Coins)	2820 (3 Coins)	9400 (10 Coins)
4000 (5 Coins)	2400 (3 Coins)	8000 (10 Coins)
$ 5.95 (5 Nickels)	$ 3.57 (3 Nickels)	$ 11.90 (10 Nickels)
29.73 (5 Quarters)	17.84 (3 Quarters)	59.46 (10 Quarters)
118.93 (5 Dollars)	71.36 (3 Dollars)	237.86 (10 Dollars)
$ 129.46 (5 Nickels)	$ 77.68 (3 Nickels)	$ 258.92 (10 Nickels)
647.30 (5 Quarters)	388.38 (3 Quarters)	1,294.60 (10 Quarters)
2,589.20 (5 Dollars)	1,553.52 (3 Dollars)	5,178.40 (10 Dollars)

Appendix C

Joker Poker Strategy Tables

The following pages contain tables of computer-generated statistics and playing strategies for nineteen distinct versions of Joker Poker. The tables are matched to the machines by way of the payoff charts on the machines. For a detailed discussion of the information on these tables, refer back to Chapter 5, "Interpreting the Strategy Tables and Cards."

JOKER WILD TWO PAIR OR BETTER TABLES
20-8-7-6 MACHINE

Payoff Table

Final Hand	1 Coin	5 Coins
Royal Flush	500	5000
Five of a Kind	100	(5 X 100)
Straight Flush*	50	(5 X 50)
Four of a Kind	20	(5 X 20)
Full House	8	(5 X 8)
Flush	7	(5 X 7)
Straight	6	(5 X 6)
Three of a Kind	2	(5 X 2)
Two Pair	1	(5 X 1)

* Joker Royal Flush counts as Straight Flush.

Long-Term Machine Payback

Fixed Royal Flush Payoff	Machine Payback
5000 (5 Coins)	102.0%
4700 (5 Coins)	101.9%
4000 (5 Coins)	101.6%
500 (1 Coin)	101.0%

Minimum Progressive Royal Flush
Jackpot Needed for 100% Machine Payback

$ 5.95 (5 Nickels)
29.73 (5 Quarters)
118.93 (5 Dollars)

Minimum Progressive Royal Flush
Jackpot Needed for 101% Machine Payback

$ 129.46 (5 Nickels)
647.30 (5 Quarters)
2,589.20 (5 Dollars)

Short-Term Win/Loss Odds

Odds of Winning	Odds of Losing
45%	55%

Playing Strategy

Joker Hand	Example	Regular Hand	Example
j5K	j 9H 9C 9D 9S	RF	AH KH QH JH TH
jRF	j AH KH QH JH	SF	9H 8H 7H 6H 5H
jSF	j 9H 8H 7H 6H	4CRF	KH QH JH TH
j4K	j 9H 9C 9D	4K	9H 9C 9D 9S
jFH	j 9H 9C 8D 8S	FH	9H 9C 8D 8S 8H
jFL	j 9H 7H 5H 3H	FL	9H 7H 5H 3H 2H
j4CRF (Qh)	j QH JH TH	ST	9H 8C 7D 6S 5H
j4CSF (O)	j 9H 8H 7H	4CSF	9H 8H 7H 6H
jST	j 9H 8C 7D 6S	3K	9H 9C 9D
j4CRF (Kh)	j KH QH JH	3CRF (Qh)	QH JH TH
j4CSF (I)	j 9H 8H — 6H	2P	9H 9C 8D 8S
j4CRF (Ah)	j AH KH QH	3CRF (Kh)	KH QH JH
j4CSF (D)	j 9H 8H — — 5H	4CFL	9H 7H 5H 3H
j3K	j 9H 9C	3CRF (Ah)	AH KH QH
j4CST (O)	j 9H 8C 7D	4CST (O)	9H 8C 7D 6S
j3CRF (Jh)	j JH TH	3CSF (O)	9H 8H 7H
j3CSF (O)	j 9H 8H	3CSF (I)	9H 8H — 6H
j4CST (I)	j 9H 8C — 6D	LP	9H 9C
j4CFL	j 9H 6H 3H	4CST (I)	9H 8C — 6D 5S
j3CRF (Qh)	j QH JH	3CSF (D)	9H 8H — — 5H
j3CSF (I)	j 9H — 7H	2CRF (Jh)	JH TH
j3CRF (Kh)	j KH QH	3CFL	9H 5H 2H
j3CSF (D)	j 9H — — 6H	3CST (O)	9H 8C 7D
j3CST (O)	j 9H 8C	2CRF (Qh)	QH JH
j4CST (D)	j 9H 8C — — 5D	2CSF (O)	9H 8H
j3CRF (Ah)	j AH KH	2CRF (Kh)	KH QH
j3CSF (Y)	j 9H — — — 5H	2CSF (I)	9H — 7H
jLP (T)	j TH	2CRF (Ah)	AH KH
j3CST (I)	j 9H — 7C	2CSF (D)	9H — — 6H
jLP (9-5)	j 9H	3CST (I)	9H 8C — 6D
jLP (J)	j JH	2CSF (Y)	9H — — — 5H
jLP (Q)	j QH	2CST (O)	9H 8C
		Draw Five	QH 9C 6D 4S 2H

(2P 20-8-7-6)

Symbol Key

j : Joker	O : Open-ended
RF : Royal Flush	I : Inside
SF : Straight Flush	D : Double-Inside
FH : Full House	Y : Triple-Inside
FL : Flush	
ST : Straight	
2P : Two Pair	
LP : Low Pair (Usually A-2, Aces to Twos)	
MC : Middle Card	

5K,4K,etc. : 5 of a Kind, 4 of a Kind, etc.
4C,3C,etc. : 4-Card, 3-Card, etc.
Ah,Kh,etc. : Ace-high, King-high, etc.

Example

j4CST (D) : Joker 4-Card Straight, Double-Inside

JOKER WILD TWO PAIR OR BETTER TABLES
20-10-6-5 MACHINE

Payoff Table

Final Hand	1 Coin	5 Coins
Royal Flush	500	5000
Five of a Kind	100	(5 X 100)
Straight Flush*	50	(5 X 50)
Four of a Kind	20	(5 X 20)
Full House	10	(5 X 10)
Flush	6	(5 X 6)
Straight	5	(5 X 5)
Three of a Kind	2	(5 X 2)
Two Pair	1	(5 X 1)

* Joker Royal Flush counts as Straight Flush.

Long-Term Machine Payback

Fixed Royal Flush Payoff	Machine Payback
5000 (5 Coins)	99.8%
4700 (5 Coins)	99.7%
4000 (5 Coins)	99.4%
500 (1 Coin)	98.7%

Minimum Progressive Royal Flush
Jackpot Needed for 100% Machine Payback

$ 270.01 (5 Nickels)
  1,350.04 (5 Quarters)
  5,400.16 (5 Dollars)

Minimum Progressive Royal Flush
Jackpot Needed for 101% Machine Payback

$ 378.10 (5 Nickels)
  1,890.52 (5 Quarters)
  7,562.09 (5 Dollars)

Short-Term Win/Loss Odds

Odds of Winning	Odds of Losing
42%	58%

Playing Strategy

Joker Hand	Example	Regular Hand	Example
j5K	j 9H 9C 9D 9S	RF	AH KH QH JH TH
jRF	j AH KH QH JH	SF	9H 8H 7H 6H 5H
jSF	j 9H 8H 7H 6H	4CRF	KH QH JH TH
j4K	j 9H 9C 9D	4K	9H 9C 9D 9S
jFH	j 9H 9C 8D 8S	FH	9H 9C 8D 8S 8H
j4CRF (Qh)	j QH JH TH	FL	9H 7H 5H 3H 2H
j4CSF (O)	j 9H 8H 7H	ST	9H 8C 7D 6S 5H
jFL	j 9H 7H 5H 3H	4CSF	9H 8H 7H 6H
j4CRF (Kh)	j KH QH JH	3K	9H 9C 9D
j4CSF (I)	j 9H 8H — 6H	2P	9H 9C 8D 8S
jST	j 9H 8C 7D 6S	3CRF	QH JH TH
j4CRF (Ah)	j AH KH QH	4CFL	9H 7H 5H 3H
j4CSF (D)	j 9H 8H — — 5H	4CST (O)	9H 8C 7D 6S
j3K	j 9H 9C	3CSF (O)	9H 8H 7H
j4CST (O)	j 9H 8C 7D	LP	9H 9C
j3CRF (Jh)	j JH TH	3CSF (I)	9H 8H — 6H
j3CSF (O)	j 9H 8H	3CSF (D)	9H 8H — — 5H
j3CRF (Qh)	j QH JH	4CST (I)	9H 8C — 6D 5S
j3CSF (I)	j 9H — 7H	2CRF (Jh)	JH TH
j4CFL	j 9H 6H 3H	2CRF (Qh)	QH JH
j4CST (I)	j 9H 8C — 6D	3CFL	9H 5H 2H
j3CRF (Kh)	j KH QH	2CSF (O)	9H 8H
j3CSF (D)	j 9H — — 6H	2CRF (Kh)	KH QH
j3CST (O)	j 9H 8C	3CST (O)	9H 8C 7D
j3CRF (Ah)	j AH KH	2CSF (I)	9H — 7H
j3CSF (Y)	j 9H — — — 5H	2CRF (Ah)	AH KH
jLP (T)	j TH	2CSF (D)	9H — — 6H
jLP (9-5)	j 9H	1CRF (T)	TH
jLP (J)	j JH	3CST (I)	9H 8C — 6D
jLP (Q)	j QH	2CSF (Y)	9H — — — 5H
j4CST (D)	j 9H 8C — — 5D	Draw Five	QH 9C 6D 4S 2H

(2P 20-10-6-5)

Symbol Key

j : Joker	O : Open-ended
RF : Royal Flush	I : Inside
SF : Straight Flush	D : Double-Inside
FH : Full House	Y : Triple-Inside
FL : Flush	
ST : Straight	
2P : Two Pair	
LP : Low Pair (Usually A-2, Aces to Twos)	
MC : Middle Card	

5K,4K,etc. : 5 of a Kind, 4 of a Kind, etc.
4C,3C,etc. : 4-Card, 3-Card, etc.
Ah,Kh,etc. : Ace-high, King-high, etc.

Example

j4CST (D) : Joker 4-Card Straight, Double-Inside

JOKER WILD TWO PAIR OR BETTER TABLES
20-8-7-5 MACHINE

Payoff Table

Final Hand	1 Coin	5 Coins
Royal Flush	500	5000
Five of a Kind	100	(5 X 100)
Straight Flush*	50	(5 X 50)
Four of a Kind	20	(5 X 20)
Full House	8	(5 X 8)
Flush	7	(5 X 7)
Straight	5	(5 X 5)
Three of a Kind	2	(5 X 2)
Two Pair	1	(5 X 1)

* Joker Royal Flush counts as Straight Flush.

Long-Term Machine Payback

Fixed Royal Flush Payoff	Machine Payback
5000 (5 Coins)	99.0%
4700 (5 Coins)	98.9%
4000 (5 Coins)	98.6%
500 (1 Coin)	98.0%

Minimum Progressive Royal Flush
Jackpot Needed for 100% Machine Payback

$ 373.45 (5 Nickels)
  1,867.27 (5 Quarters)
  7,469.08 (5 Dollars)

Minimum Progressive Royal Flush
Jackpot Needed for 101% Machine Payback

$ 495.77 (5 Nickels)
  2,478.83 (5 Quarters)
  9,915.31 (5 Dollars)

Short-Term Win/Loss Odds

Odds of Winning	Odds of Losing
41%	59%

Playing Strategy

Joker Hand	Example	Regular Hand	Example
j5K	j 9H 9C 9D 9S	RF	AH KH QH JH TH
jRF	j AH KH QH JH	SF	9H 8H 7H 6H 5H
jSF	j 9H 8H 7H 6H	4CRF	KH QH JH TH
j4K	j 9H 9C 9D	4K	9H 9C 9D 9S
jFH	j 9H 9C 8D 8S	FH	9H 9C 8D 8S 8H
jFL	j 9H 7H 5H 3H	FL	9H 7H 5H 3H 2H
j4CRF (Qh)	j QH JH TH	ST	9H 8C 7D 6S 5H
j4CSF (O)	j 9H 8H 7H	4CSF	9H 8H 7H 6H
j4CRF (Kh)	j KH QH JH	3K	9H 9C 9D
j4CSF (I)	j 9H 8H — 6H	3CRF (Qh)	QH JH TH
jST	j 9H 8C 7D 6S	2P	9H 9C 8D 8S
j4CRF (Ah)	j AH KH QH	3CRF (Kh)	KH QH JH
j4CSF (D)	j 9H 8H — — 5H	4CFL	9H 7H 5H 3H
j3K	j 9H 9C	3CRF (Ah)	AH KH QH
j4CST (O)	j 9H 8C 7D	4CST (O)	9H 8C 7D 6S
j3CRF (Jh)	j JH TH	3CSF (O)	9H 8H 7H
j3CSF (O)	j 9H 8H	3CSF (I)	9H 8H — 6H
j4CFL	j 9H 6H 3H	LP	9H 9C
j3CRF (Qh)	j QH JH	3CSF (D)	9H 8H — — 5H
j3CSF (I)	j 9H — 7H	4CST (I)	9H 8C — 6D 5S
j4CST (I)	j 9H 8C — 6D	2CRF (Jh)	JH TH
j3CRF (Kh)	j KH QH	3CFL	9H 5H 2H
j3CSF (D)	j 9H — — 6H	2CRF (Qh)	QH JH
j3CRF (Ah)	j AH KH	2CSF (O)	9H 8H
j3CSF (Y)	j 9H — — — 5H	2CRF (Kh)	KH QH
j3CST (O)	j 9H 8C	3CST (O)	9H 8C 7D
jLP (T)	j TH	2CSF (I)	9H — 7H
jLP (J)	j JH	2CRF (Ah)	AH KH
jLP (9-5)	j 9H	2CSF (D)	9H — — 6H
jLP (Q)	j QH	2CSF (Y)	9H — — — 5H
j4CST (D)	j 9H 8C — — 5D	1CRF (T)	TH
		3CST (I)	9H 8C — 6D
		Draw Five	QH 9C 6D 4S 2H

(2P 20-8-7-5)

Symbol Key

      j : Joker   O : Open-ended
     RF : Royal Flush   I : Inside
     SF : Straight Flush   D : Double-Inside
     FH : Full House   Y : Triple-Inside
     FL : Flush
     ST : Straight
     2P : Two Pair
     LP : Low Pair (Usually A-2, Aces to Twos)
     MC : Middle Card

     5K,4K,etc. : 5 of a Kind, 4 of a Kind, etc.
     4C,3C,etc. : 4-Card, 3-Card, etc.
     Ah,Kh,etc. : Ace-high, King-high, etc.

Example

     j4CST (D) : Joker 4-Card Straight, Double-Inside

JOKER WILD TWO PAIR OR BETTER TABLES
16-8-5-4 MACHINE

Payoff Table

Final Hand	1 Coin	5 Coins
Five of a Kind	400	4000
Straight Flush*	100	(5 X 100)
Four of a Kind	16	(5 X 16)
Full House	8	(5 X 8)
Flush	5	(5 X 5)
Straight	4	(5 X 4)
Three of a Kind	2	(5 X 2)
Two Pair	1	(5 X 1)

* Regular Royal Flush and Joker Royal Flush
  counts as Straight Flush.

Long-Term Machine Payback

Fixed Five of a Kind Payoff	Machine Payback
5000 (5 Coins)	98.9%
4700 (5 Coins)	98.3%
4000 (5 Coins)	97.1%
400 (1 Coin)	93.4%

Minimum Progressive Five of a Kind
Jackpot Needed for 100% Machine Payback

$ 280.46 (5 Nickels)
   1,402.32 (5 Quarters)
   5,609.29 (5 Dollars)

Minimum Progressive Five of a Kind
Jackpot Needed for 101% Machine Payback

$ 308.01 (5 Nickels)
   1,540.05 (5 Quarters)
   6,160.18 (5 Dollars)

Short-Term Win/Loss Odds

Odds of Winning	Odds of Losing
25%	75%

Playing Strategy

Joker Hand	Example	Regular Hand	Example
j5K	j 9H 9C 9D 9S	RF	AH KH QH JH TH
jRF	j AH KH QH JH	SF	9H 8H 7H 6H 5H
jSF	j 9H 8H 7H 6H	4K	9H 9C 9D 9S
j4K	j 9H 9C 9D	FH	9H 9C 8D 8S 8H
j4CRF (Qh)	j QH JH TH	4CRF (Kh)	KH QH JH TH
j4CSF (O)	j 9H 8H 7H	4CSF (O)	9H 8H 7H 6H
j4CRF (Kh)	j KH QH JH	4CRF (Ah)	AH KH QH JH
j4CSF (I)	j 9H 8H — 6H	4CSF (I)	9H 8H — 6H 5H
jFH	j 9H 9C 8D 8S	FL	9H 7H 5H 3H 2H
j4CRF (Ah)	j AH KH QH	3K	9H 9C 9D
j4CSF (D)	j 9H 8H — — 5H	ST	9H 8C 7D 6S 5H
jFL	j 9H 7H 5H 3H	2P	9H 9C 8D 8S
j3K	j 9H 9C	3CRF (Qh)	QH JH TH
jST	j 9H 8C 7D 6S	3CSF (O)	9H 8H 7H
j3CRF (Jh)	j JH TH	4CFL	9H 7H 5H 3H
j3CSF (O)	j 9H 8H	3CRF (Kh)	KH QH JH
j3CRF (Qh)	j QH JH	3CSF (I)	9H 8H — 6H
j3CSF (I)	j 9H — 7H	4CST (O)	9H 8C 7D 6S
j4CST (O)	j 9H 8C 7D	LP	9H 9C
j3CRF (Kh)	j KH QH	3CRF (Ah)	AH KH QH
j3CSF (D)	j 9H — — 6H	3CSF (D)	9H 8H — — 5H
j4CFL	j 9H 6H 3H	4CST (I)	9H 8C — 6D 5S
j4CST (I)	j 9H 8C — 6D	2CRF (Jh)	JH TH
j3CRF (Ah)	j AH KH	2CSF (O)	9H 8H
j3CSF (Y)	j 9H — — — 5H	3CFL	9H 5H 2H
jLP (T)	j TH	2CRF (Qh)	QH JH
jLP (9-5)	j 9H	2CSF (I)	9H — 7H
jLP (J)	j JH	3CST (O)	9H 8C 7D
j3CST (O)	j 9H 8C	2CRF (Kh)	KH QH
jLP (Q)	j QH	2CSF (D)	9H — — 6H
jDraw Four	j QH JC 3D 2S	1CRF (T)	TH
		2CRF (Ah)	AH KH
		2CSF (Y)	9H — — — 5H
		1MC (9-5)	9H
		Draw Five	QH 9C 6D 4S 2H

(2P 16-8-5-4)

Symbol Key

```
         j : Joker              O : Open-ended
        RF : Royal Flush        I : Inside
        SF : Straight Flush     D : Double-Inside
        FH : Full House         Y : Triple-Inside
        FL : Flush
        ST : Straight
        2P : Two Pair
        LP : Low Pair (Usually A-2, Aces to Twos)
        MC : Middle Card

        5K,4K,etc. : 5 of a Kind, 4 of a Kind, etc.
        4C,3C,etc. : 4-Card, 3-Card, etc.
        Ah,Kh,etc. : Ace-high, King-high, etc.
```
Example
```
        j4CST (D) : Joker 4-Card Straight, Double-Inside
```

JOKER WILD TWO PAIR OR BETTER TABLES
20-8-6-5 MACHINE

Payoff Table

Final Hand	1 Coin	5 Coins
Royal Flush	500	5000
Five of a Kind	100	(5 X 100)
Straight Flush*	50	(5 X 50)
Four of a Kind	20	(5 X 20)
Full House	8	(5 X 8)
Flush	6	(5 X 6)
Straight	5	(5 X 5)
Three of a Kind	2	(5 X 2)
Two Pair	1	(5 X 1)

* Joker Royal Flush counts as Straight Flush.

Long-Term Machine Payback

Fixed Royal Flush Payoff	Machine Payback
5000 (5 Coins)	96.8%
4700 (5 Coins)	96.7%
4000 (5 Coins)	96.4%
500 (1 Coin)	95.7%

Minimum Progressive Royal Flush
Jackpot Needed for 100% Machine Payback

$ 593.76	(5 Nickels)
2,968.79	(5 Quarters)
11,875.18	(5 Dollars)

Minimum Progressive Royal Flush
Jackpot Needed for 101% Machine Payback

$ 701.95	(5 Nickels)
3,509.75	(5 Quarters)
14,039.01	(5 Dollars)

Short-Term Win/Loss Odds

Odds of Winning	Odds of Losing
37%	63%

Playing Strategy

Joker Hand	Example	Regular Hand	Example
j5K	j 9H 9C 9D 9S	RF	AH KH QH JH TH
jRF	j AH KH QH JH	SF	9H 8H 7H 6H 5H
jSF	j 9H 8H 7H 6H	4CRF	KH QH JH TH
j4K	j 9H 9C 9D	4K	9H 9C 9D 9S
jFH	j 9H 9C 8D 8S	FH	9H 9C 8D 8S 8H
j4CRF (Qh)	j QH JH TH	FL	9H 7H 5H 3H 2H
j4CSF (O)	j 9H 8H 7H	ST	9H 8C 7D 6S 5H
jFL	j 9H 7H 5H 3H	4CSF	9H 8H 7H 6H
j4CRF (Kh)	j KH QH JH	3K	9H 9C 9D
j4CSF (I)	j 9H 8H — 6H	2P	9H 9C 8D 8S
jST	j 9H 8C 7D 6S	3CRF	QH JH TH
j4CRF (Ah)	j AH KH QH	4CFL	9H 7H 5H 3H
j4CSF (D)	j 9H 8H — — 5H	4CST (O)	9H 8C 7D 6S
j3K	j 9H 9C	3CSF (O)	9H 8H 7H
j4CST (O)	j 9H 8C 7D	LP	9H 9C
j3CRF (Jh)	j JH TH	3CSF (I)	9H 8H — 6H
j3CSF (O)	j 9H 8H	3CSF (D)	9H 8H — — 5H
j3CRF (Qh)	j QH JH	4CST (I)	9H 8C — 6D 5S
j3CSF (I)	j 9H — 7H	2CRF (Jh)	JH TH
j4CFL	j 9H 6H 3H	2CRF (Qh)	QH JH
j4CST (I)	j 9H 8C — 6D	3CFL	9H 5H 2H
j3CRF (Kh)	j KH QH	2CSF (O)	9H 8H
j3CSF (D)	j 9H — — 6H	3CST (O)	9H 8C 7D
j3CST (O)	j 9H 8C	2CRF (Kh)	KH QH
j3CRF (Ah)	j AH KH	2CSF (I)	9H — 7H
j3CSF (Y)	j 9H — — — 5H	2CRF (Ah)	AH KH
jLP (T)	j TH	2CSF (D)	9H — — 6H
jLP (9-5)	j 9H	1CRF (T)	TH
jLP (J)	j JH	3CST (I)	9H 8C — 6D
j4CST (D)	j 9H 8C — — 5D	2CSF (Y)	9H — — — 5H
jLP (Q)	j QH	Draw Five	QH 9C 6D 4S 2H

(2P 20-8-6-5)

Symbol Key

j : Joker	O : Open-ended
RF : Royal Flush	I : Inside
SF : Straight Flush	D : Double-Inside
FH : Full House	Y : Triple-Inside
FL : Flush	
ST : Straight	
2P : Two Pair	
LP : Low Pair (Usually A-2, Aces to Twos)	
MC : Middle Card	

5K,4K,etc. : 5 of a Kind, 4 of a Kind, etc.
4C,3C,etc. : 4-Card, 3-Card, etc.
Ah,Kh,etc. : Ace-high, King-high, etc.

Example

j4CST (D) : Joker 4-Card Straight, Double-Inside

JOKER WILD TWO PAIR OR BETTER TABLES
25-8-5-4 MACHINE

Payoff Table

Final Hand	1 Coin	5 Coins
Royal Flush	500	5000
Five of a Kind	100	(5 X 100)
Straight Flush*	50	(5 X 50)
Four of a Kind	25	(5 X 25)
Full House	8	(5 X 8)
Flush	5	(5 X 5)
Straight	4	(5 X 4)
Three of a Kind	2	(5 X 2)
Two Pair	1	(5 X 1)

* Joker Royal Flush counts as Straight Flush.

Long-Term Machine Payback

Fixed Royal Flush Payoff	Machine Payback
5000 (5 Coins)	96.0%
4700 (5 Coins)	95.9%
4000 (5 Coins)	95.6%
500 (1 Coin)	94.9%

Minimum Progressive Royal Flush
Jackpot Needed for 100% Machine Payback

$ 676.94 (5 Nickels)
3,384.68 (5 Quarters)
15,538.71 (5 Dollars)

Minimum Progressive Royal Flush
Jackpot Needed for 101% Machine Payback

$ 784.72 (5 Nickels)
3,923.59 (5 Quarters)
15,694.36 (5 Dollars)

Short-Term Win/Loss Odds

Odds of Winning	Odds of Losing
37%	63%

Playing Strategy

Joker Hand	Example	Regular Hand	Example
j5K	j 9H 9C 9D 9S	RF	AH KH QH JH TH
jRF	j AH KH QH JH	SF	9H 8H 7H 6H 5H
jSF	j 9H 8H 7H 6H	4K	9H 9C 9D 9S
j4K	j 9H 9C 9D	4CRF	KH QH JH TH
jFH	j 9H 9C 8D 8S	FH	9H 9C 8D 8S 8H
j4CRF (Qh)	j QH JH TH	FL	9H 7H 5H 3H 2H
j4CSF (O)	j 9H 8H 7H	4CSF (O)	9H 8H 7H 6H
jFL	j 9H 7H 5H 3H	3K	9H 9C 9D
j4CRF (Kh)	j KH QH JH	ST	9H 8C 7D 6S 5H
j4CSF (I)	j 9H 8H — 6H	4CSF (I)	9H 8H — 6H 5H
j3K	j 9H 9C	2P	9H 9C 8D 8S
jST	j 9H 8C 7D 6S	3CRF	QH JH TH
j4CRF (Ah)	j AH KH QH	4CFL	9H 7H 5H 3H
j4CSF (D)	j 9H 8H — — 5H	3CSF (O)	9H 8H 7H
j3CRF (Jh)	j JH TH	LP	9H 9C
j3CSF (O)	j 9H 8H	4CST (O)	9H 8C 7D 6S
j4CST (O)	j 9H 8C 7D	3CSF (I)	9H 8H — 6H
j3CRF (Qh)	j QH JH	3CSF (D)	9H 8H — — 5H
j3CSF (I)	j 9H — 7H	4CST (I)	9H 8C — 6D 5S
j4CFL	j 9H 6H 3H	2CRF (Jh)	JH TH
j3CRF (Kh)	j KH QH	2CRF (Qh)	QH JH
j3CSF (D)	j 9H — — 6H	2CSF (O)	9H 8H
j4CST (I)	j 9H 8C — 6D	3CFL	9H 5H 2H
jLP (T)	j TH	2CRF (Kh)	KH QH
j3CRF (Ah)	j AH KH	2CSF (I)	9H — 7H
j3CSF (Y)	j 9H — — — 5H	2CRF (Ah)	AH KH
jLP (9-5)	j 9H	3CST (O)	9H 8C 7D
jLP (J)	j JH	2CSF (D)	9H — — 6H
j3CST (O)	j 9H 8C	1CRF (T)	TH
jLP (Q)	j QH	Draw Five	QH 9C 6D 4S 2H
jDraw Four	j QH JC 3D 2S		

(2P 25-8-5-4)

Symbol Key

j : Joker   O : Open-ended
RF : Royal Flush   I : Inside
SF : Straight Flush   D : Double-Inside
FH : Full House   Y : Triple-Inside
FL : Flush
ST : Straight
2P : Two Pair
LP : Low Pair (Usually A-2, Aces to Twos)
MC : Middle Card

5K,4K,etc. : 5 of a Kind, 4 of a Kind, etc.
4C,3C,etc. : 4-Card, 3-Card, etc.
Ah,Kh,etc. : Ace-high, King-high, etc.

Example

j4CST (D) : Joker 4-Card Straight, Double-Inside

JOKER WILD TWO PAIR OR BETTER TABLES
20-8-6-4 MACHINE

Payoff Table

Final Hand	1 Coin	5 Coins
Royal Flush	500	5000
Five of a Kind	100	(5 X 100)
Straight Flush*	50	(5 X 50)
Four of a Kind	20	(5 X 20)
Full House	8	(5 X 8)
Flush	6	(5 X 6)
Straight	4	(5 X 4)
Three of a Kind	2	(5 X .2)
Two Pair	1	(5 X 1)

* Joker Royal Flush counts as Straight Flush.

Long-Term Machine Payback

Fixed Royal Flush Payoff	Machine Payback
5000 (5 Coins)	94.0%
4700 (5 Coins)	93.9%
4000 (5 Coins)	93.6%
500 (1 Coin)	92.9%

Minimum Progressive Royal Flush
Jackpot Needed for 100% Machine Payback

$ 902.69 (5 Nickels)
4,513.44 (5 Quarters)
18,053.78 (5 Dollars)

Minimum Progressive Royal Flush
Jackpot Needed for 101% Machine Payback

$ 1,012.31 (5 Nickels)
5,061.55 (5 Quarters)
20,246.18 (5 Dollars)

Short-Term Win/Loss Odds

Odds of Winning	Odds of Losing
32%	68%

Playing Strategy

Joker Hand	Example	Regular Hand	Example
j5K	j 9H 9C 9D 9S	RF	AH KH QH JH TH
jRF	j AH KH QH JH	SF	9H 8H 7H 6H 5H
jSF	j 9H 8H 7H 6H	4CRF	KH QH JH TH
j4K	j 9H 9C 9D	4K	9H 9C 9D 9S
jFH	j 9H 9C 8D 8S	FH	9H 9C 8D 8S 8H
j4CRF (Qh)	j QH JH TH	FL	9H 7H 5H 3H 2H
j4CSF (O)	j 9H 8H 7H	4CSF (O)	9H 8H 7H 6H
jFL	j 9H 7H 5H 3H	ST	9H 8C 7D 6S 5H
j4CRF (Kh)	j KH QH JH	3K	9H 9C 9D
j4CSF (I)	j 9H 8H — 6H	4CSF (I)	9H 8H — 6H 5H
jST	j 9H 8C 7D 6S	2P	9H 9C 8D 8S
j4CRF (Ah)	j AH KH QH	3CRF	QH JH TH
j4CSF (D)	j 9H 8H — — 5H	4CFL	9H 7H 5H 3H
j3K	j 9H 9C	3CSF (O)	9H 8H 7H
j3CRF (Jh)	j JH TH	4CST (O)	9H 8C 7D 6S
j3CSF (O)	j 9H 8H	LP	9H 9C
j4CST (O)	j 9H 8C 7D	3CSF (I)	9H 8H — 6H
j4CFL	j 9H 6H 3H	3CSF (D)	9H 8H — — 5H
j3CRF (Qh)	j QH JH	4CST (I)	9H 8C — 6D 5S
j3CSF (I)	j 9H — 7H	2CRF (Jh)	JH TH
j3CRF (Kh)	j KH QH	3CFL	9H 5H 2H
j3CSF (D)	j 9H — — 6H	2CRF (Qh)	QH JH
j4CST (I)	j 9H 8C — 6D	2CSF (O)	9H 8H
j3CRF (Ah)	j AH KH	2CRF (Kh)	KH QH
j3CSF (Y)	j 9H — — — 5H	2CSF (I)	9H — 7H
jLP (T)	j TH	2CRF (Ah)	AH KH
j3CST (O)	j 9H 8C	3CST (O)	9H 8C 7D
jLP (J)	j JH	2CSF (D)	9H — — 6H
jLP (9-5)	j 9H	1CRF (T)	TH
jLP (Q)	j QH	2CSF (Y)	9H — — — 5H
jDraw Four	j QH JC 3D 2S	Draw Five	QH 9C 6D 4S 2H

(2P 20-8-6-4)

Symbol Key

j : Joker	O : Open-ended
RF : Royal Flush	I : Inside
SF : Straight Flush	D : Double-Inside
FH : Full House	Y : Triple-Inside
FL : Flush	
ST : Straight	
2P : Two Pair	
LP : Low Pair (Usually A-2, Aces to Twos)	
MC : Middle Card	

5K,4K,etc. : 5 of a Kind, 4 of a Kind, etc.
4C,3C,etc. : 4-Card, 3-Card, etc.
Ah,Kh,etc. : Ace-high, King-high, etc.

Example

j4CST (D) : Joker 4-Card Straight, Double-Inside

JOKER WILD TWO PAIR OR BETTER TABLES
15-6-5-4 MACHINE

Payoff Table

Final Hand	1 Coin	5 Coins
Five of a Kind	400	4000
Straight Flush*	100	(5 X 100)
Four of a Kind	15	(5 X 15)
Full House	6	(5 X 6)
Flush	5	(5 X 5)
Straight	4	(5 X 4)
Three of a Kind	2	(5 X 2)
Two Pair	1	(5 X 1)

* Regular Royal Flush and Joker Royal Flush
  count as Straight Flushes.

Long-Term Machine Payback

Fixed Five of a Kind Payoff	Machine Payback
5000 (5 Coins)	95.1%
4700 (5 Coins)	94.5%
4000 (5 Coins)	93.3%
400 (1 Coin)	89.6%

Minimum Progressive Five of a Kind
Jackpot Needed for 100% Machine Payback

$ 386.04 (5 Nickels)
  1,930.19 (5 Quarters)
  7,720.77 (5 Dollars)

Minimum Progressive Five of a Kind
Jackpot Needed for 101% Machine Payback

$ 413.60 (5 Nickels)
  2,068.01 (5 Quarters)
  8,272.05 (5 Dollars)

Short-Term Win/Loss Odds

Odds of Winning	Odds of Losing
20%	80%

Playing Strategy

Joker Hand	Example	Regular Hand	Example
j5K	j 9H 9C 9D 9S	RF	AH KH QH JH TH
jRF	j AH KH QH JH	SF	9H 8H 7H 6H 5H
jSF	j 9H 8H 7H 6H	4K	9H 9C 9D 9S
j4K	j 9H 9C 9D	4CRF (Kh)	KH QH JH TH
j4CRF (Qh)	j QH JH TH	4CSF (O)	9H 8H 7H 6H
j4CSF (O)	j 9H 8H 7H	FH	9H 9C 8D 8S 8H
j4CRF (Kh)	j KH QH JH	4CRF (Ah)	AH KH QH JH
j4CSF (I)	j 9H 8H — 6H	4CSF (I)	9H 8H — 6H 5H
jFH	j 9H 9C 8D 8S	FL	9H 7H 5H 3H 2H
j4CRF (Ah)	j AH KH QH	3K	9H 9C 9D
j4CSF (D)	j 9H 8H — — 5H	ST	9H 8C 7D 6S 5H
jFL	j 9H 7H 5H 3H	2P	9H 9C 8D 8S
j3K	j 9H 9C	3CRF (Qh)	QH JH TH
jST	j 9H 8C 7D 6S	3CSF (O)	9H 8H 7H
j3CRF (Jh)	j JH TH	4CFL	9H 7H 5H 3H
j3CSF (O)	j 9H 8H	3CRF (Kh)	KH QH JH
j3CRF (Qh)	j QH JH	3CSF (I)	9H 8H — 6H
j3CSF (I)	j 9H — 7H	4CST (O)	9H 8C 7D 6S
j4CST (O)	j 9H 8C 7D	LP	9H 9C
j3CRF (Kh)	j KH QH	3CRF (Ah)	AH KH QH
j3CSF (D)	j 9H — — 6H	3CSF (D)	9H 8H — — 5H
j4CFL	j 9H 6H 3H	4CST (I)	9H 8C — 6D 5S
j4CST (I)	j 9H 8C — 6D	2CRF (Jh)	JH TH
j3CRF (Ah)	j AH KH	2CSF (O)	9H 8H
j3CSF (Y)	j 9H — — — 5H	3CFL	9H 5H 2H
jLP (T)	j TH	2CRF (Qh)	QH JH
jLP (9-5)	j 9H	2CSF (I)	9H — 7H
jLP (J)	j JH	3CST (O)	9H 8C 7D
j3CST (O)	j 9H 8C	2CRF (Kh)	KH QH
jLP (Q)	j QH	2CSF (D)	9H — — 6H
jDraw Four	j QH JC 3D 2S	2CRF (Ah)	AH KH
		2CSF (Y)	9H — — — 5H
		1CRF (T)	TH
		1MC (9-5)	9H
		Draw Five	QH 9C 6D 4S 2H

(2P 15-6-5-4)

Symbol Key

j : Joker	O : Open-ended
RF : Royal Flush	I : Inside
SF : Straight Flush	D : Double-Inside
FH : Full House	Y : Triple-Inside
FL : Flush	
ST : Straight	
2P : Two Pair	
LP : Low Pair (Usually A-2, Aces to Twos)	
MC : Middle Card	

5K,4K,etc. : 5 of a Kind, 4 of a Kind, etc.
4C,3C,etc. : 4-Card, 3-Card, etc.
Ah,Kh,etc. : Ace-high, King-high, etc.

Example

j4CST (D) : Joker 4-Card Straight, Double-Inside

JOKER WILD TWO PAIR OR BETTER TABLES
20-8-5-4 MACHINE

Payoff Table

Final Hand	1 Coin	5 Coins
Royal Flush	500	5000
Five of a Kind	100	(5 X 100)
Straight Flush*	50	(5 X 50)
Four of a Kind	20	(5 X 20)
Full House	8	(5 X 8)
Flush	5	(5 X 5)
Straight	4	(5 X 4)
Three of a Kind	2	(5 X 2)
Two Pair	1	(5 X 1)

* Joker Royal Flush counts as Straight Flush.

Long-Term Machine Payback

Fixed Royal Flush Payoff	Machine Payback
5000 (5 Coins)	91.9%
4700 (5 Coins)	91.8%
4000 (5 Coins)	91.5%
500 (1 Coin)	90.8%

Minimum Progressive Royal Flush
Jackpot Needed for 100% Machine Payback

$ 1,121.41 (5 Nickels)
5,607.05 (5 Quarters)
22,428.20 (5 Dollars)

Minimum Progressive Royal Flush
Jackpot Needed for 101% Machine Payback

$ 1,229.19 (5 Nickels)
6,145.96 (5 Quarters)
24,583.85 (5 Dollars)

Short-Term Win/Loss Odds

Odds of Winning	Odds of Losing
30%	70%

Playing Strategy

Joker Hand	Example	Regular Hand	Example
j5K	j 9H 9C 9D 9S	RF	AH KH QH JH TH
jRF	j AH KH QH JH	SF	9H 8H 7H 6H 5H
jSF	j 9H 8H 7H 6H	4CRF	KH QH JH TH
j4K	j 9H 9C 9D	4K	9H 9C 9D 9S
jFH	j 9H 9C 8D 8S	FH	9H 9C 8D 8S 8H
j4CRF (Qh)	j QH JH TH	FL	9H 7H 5H 3H 2H
j4CSF (O)	j 9H 8H 7H	4CSF (O)	9H 8H 7H 6H
jFL	j 9H 7H 5H 3H	ST	9H 8C 7D 6S 5H
j4CRF (Kh)	j KH QH JH	3K	9H 9C 9D
j4CSF (I)	j 9H 8H — 6H	4CSF (I)	9H 8H — 6H 5H
jST	j 9H 8C 7D 6S	2P	9H 9C 8D 8S
j3K	j 9H 9C	3CRF	QH JH TH
j4CRF (Ah)	j AH KH QH	4CFL	9H 7H 5H 3H
j4CSF (D)	j 9H 8H — — 5H	3CSF (O)	9H 8H 7H
j3CRF (Jh)	j JH TH	4CST (O)	9H 8C 7D 6S
j3CSF (O)	j 9H 8H	LP	9H 9C
j4CST (O)	j 9H 8C 7D	3CSF (I)	9H 8H — 6H
j3CRF (Qh)	j QH JH	3CSF (D)	9H 8H — — 5H
j3CSF (I)	j 9H — 7H	4CST (I)	9H 8C — 6D 5S
j4CFL	j 9H 6H 3H	2CRF (Jh)	JH TH
j3CRF (Kh)	j KH QH	2CRF (Qh)	QH JH
j3CSF (D)	j 9H — — 6H	2CSF (O)	9H 8H
j4CST (I)	j 9H 8C — 6D	3CFL	9H 5H 2H
j3CRF (Ah)	j AH KH	2CRF (Kh)	KH QH
j3CSF (Y)	j 9H — — — 5H	2CSF (I)	9H — 7H
jLP (T)	j TH	2CRF (Ah)	AH KH
j3CST (O)	j 9H 8C	3CST (O)	9H 8C 7D
jLP (9-5)	j 9H	2CSF (D)	9H — — 6H
jLP (J)	j JH	1CRF (T)	TH
jLP (Q)	j QH	Draw Five	QH 9C 6D 4S 2H
jDraw Four	j QH JC 3D 2S		

(2P 20-8-5-4)

Symbol Key

j : Joker	O : Open-ended
RF : Royal Flush	I : Inside
SF : Straight Flush	D : Double-Inside
FH : Full House	Y : Triple-Inside
FL : Flush	
ST : Straight	
2P : Two Pair	
LP : Low Pair (Usually A-2, Aces to Twos)	
MC : Middle Card	

5K,4K,etc. : 5 of a Kind, 4 of a Kind, etc.
4C,3C,etc. : 4-Card, 3-Card, etc.
Ah,Kh,etc. : Ace-high, King-high, etc.

Example

j4CST (D) : Joker 4-Card Straight, Double-Inside

JOKER WILD TWO PAIR OR BETTER TABLES
20-10-4-3 MACHINE

Payoff Table

Final Hand	1 Coin	5 Coins
Royal Flush	500	5000
Five of a Kind	100	(5 X 100)
Straight Flush*	50	(5 X 50)
Four of a Kind	20	(5 X 20)
Full House	10	(5 X 10)
Flush	4	(5 X 4)
Straight	3	(5 X 3)
Three of a Kind	2	(5 X 2)
Two Pair	1	(5 X 1)

* Joker Royal Flush counts as Straight Flush.

Long-Term Machine Payback

Fixed Royal Flush Payoff	Machine Payback
5000 (5 Coins)	90.4%
4700 (5 Coins)	90.3%
4000 (5 Coins)	89.9%
500 (1 Coin)	89.2%

Minimum Progressive Royal Flush
Jackpot Needed for 100% Machine Payback

$ 1,205.16 (5 Nickels)
6,025.78 (5 Quarters)
24,103.12 (5 Dollars)

Minimum Progressive Royal Flush
Jackpot Needed for 101% Machine Payback

$ 1,304.73 (5 Nickels)
6,523.63 (5 Quarters)
26,094.53 (5 Dollars)

Short-Term Win/Loss Odds

Odds of Winning	Odds of Losing
29%	71%

Playing Strategy

Joker Hand	Example	Regular Hand	Example
j5K	j 9H 9C 9D 9S	RF	AH KH QH JH TH
jRF	j AH KH QH JH	SF	9H 8H 7H 6H 5H
jSF	j 9H 8H 7H 6H	4CRF	KH QH JH TH
j4K	j 9H 9C 9D	4K	9H 9C 9D 9S
jFH	j 9H 9C 8D 8S	FH	9H 9C 8D 8S 8H
j4CRF (Qh)	j QH JH TH	3K	9H 9C 9D
j4CSF (O)	j 9H 8H 7H	FL	9H 7H 5H 3H 2H
j4CRF (Kh)	j KH QH JH	4CSF (O)	9H 8H 7H 6H
j4CSF (I)	j 9H 8H — 6H	ST	9H 8C 7D 6S 5H
j3K	j 9H 9C	4CSF (I)	9H 8H — 6H 5H
jFL	j 9H 7H 5H 3H	2P	9H 9C 8D 8S
j4CRF (Ah)	j AH KH QH	3CRF	QH JH TH
j4CSF (D)	j 9H 8H — — 5H	4CFL	9H 7H 5H 3H
jST	j 9H 8C 7D 6S	LP	9H 9C
j3CRF (Jh)	j JH TH	3CSF (O)	9H 8H 7H
j3CSF (O)	j 9H 8H	4CST (O)	9H 8C 7D 6S
j3CRF (Qh)	j QH JH	3CSF (I)	9H 8H — 6H
j3CSF (I)	j 9H — 7H	3CSF (D)	9H 8H — — 5H
j4CST (O)	j 9H 8C 7D	2CRF (Jh)	JH TH
j3CRF (Kh)	j KH QH	4CST (I)	9H 8C — 6D 5S
j3CSF (D)	j 9H — — 6H	2CRF (Qh)	QH JH
j4CFL	j 9H 6H 3H	2CRF (Kh)	KH QH
jLP (T)	j TH	2CSF (O)	9H 8H
j3CRF (Ah)	j AH KH	2CRF (Ah)	AH KH
j3CSF (Y)	j 9H — — — 5H	2CSF (I)	9H — 7H
jLP (9-5)	j 9H	3CFL	9H 5H 2H
jLP (J)	j JH	2CSF (D)	9H — — 6H
j4CST (I)	j 9H 8C — 6D	1CRF (T)	TH
jLP (Q)	j QH	Draw Five	QH 9C 6D 4S 2H
j3CST (O)	j 9H 8C		
jDraw Four	j QH JC 3D 2S		

(2P 20-10-4-3)

Symbol Key

j : Joker	O : Open-ended
RF : Royal Flush	I : Inside
SF : Straight Flush	D : Double-Inside
FH : Full House	Y : Triple-Inside
FL : Flush	
ST : Straight	
2P : Two Pair	
LP : Low Pair (Usually A-2, Aces to Twos)	
MC : Middle Card	

5K,4K,etc. : 5 of a Kind, 4 of a Kind, etc.
4C,3C,etc. : 4-Card, 3-Card, etc.
Ah,Kh,etc. : Ace-high, King-high, etc.

Example

j4CST (D) : Joker 4-Card Straight, Double-Inside

JOKER WILD TWO PAIR OR BETTER TABLES
15-6-4-3 MACHINE

Payoff Table

Final Hand	1 Coin	5 Coins
Five of a Kind	500	4000
Straight Flush *	100	(5 X 100)
Four of a Kind	15	(5 X 15)
Full House	6	(5 X 6)
Flush	4	(5 X 4)
Straight	3	(5 X 3)
Three of a Kind	2	(5 X 2)
Two Pair	1	(5 X 1)

* Regular Royal Flush and Joker Royal Flush
  count as Straight Flushes.

Long-Term Machine Payback

Fixed Five of a Kind Payoff	Machine Payback
5000 (5 Coins)	90.5%
4700 (5 Coins)	90.0%
4000 (5 Coins)	88.7%
500 (1 Coin)	86.0%

Minimum Progressive Five of a Kind
Jackpot Needed for 100% Machine Payback

$ 509.17 (5 Nickels)
   2,545.84 (5 Quarters)
  10,183.35 (5 Dollars)

Minimum Progressive Five of a Kind
Jackpot Needed for 101% Machine Payback

$ 536.53 (5 Nickels)
   2,682.66 (5 Quarters)
  10,730.65 (5 Dollars)

Short-Term Win/Loss Odds

Odds of Winning	Odds of Losing
16%	84%

Playing Strategy

Joker Hand	Example	Regular Hand	Example
j5K	j 9H 9C 9D 9S	RF	AH KH QH JH TH
jRF	j AH KH QH JH	SF	9H 8H 7H 6H 5H
jSF	j 9H 8H 7H 6H	4K	9H 9C 9D 9S
j4K	j 9H 9C 9D	4CRF (Kh)	KH QH JH TH
j4CRF (Qh)	j QH JH TH	4CSF (O)	9H 8H 7H 6H
j4CSF (O)	j 9H 8H 7H	FH	9H 9C 8D 8S 8H
j4CRF (Kh)	j KH QH JH	4CRF (Ah)	AH KH QH JH
j4CSF (I)	j 9H 8H — 6H	4CSF (I)	9H 8H — 6H 5H
jFH	j 9H 9C 8D 8S	3K	9H 9C 9D
j4CRF (Ah)	j AH KH QH	FL	9H 7H 5H 3H 2H
j4CSF (D)	j 9H 8H — — 5H	ST	9H 8C 7D 6S 5H
j3K	j 9H 9C	2P	9H 9C 8D 8S
jFL	j 9H 7H 5H 3H	3CRF (Qh)	QH JH TH
jST	j 9H 8C 7D 6S	3CSF (O)	9H 8H 7H
j3CRF (Jh)	j JH TH	4CFL	9H 7H 5H 3H
j3CRF (O)	j 9H 8H	3CRF (Kh)	KH QH JH
j3CRF (Qh)	j QH JH	3CSF (I)	9H 8H — 6H
j3CSF (I)	j 9H — 7H	LP	9H 9C
j3CRF (Kh)	j KH QH	4CST (O)	9H 8C 7D 6S
j3CSF (D)	j 9H — — 6H	3CRF (Ah)	AH KH QH
j4CST (O)	j 9H 8C 7D	3CSF (D)	9H 8H — — 5H
j3CRF (Ah)	j AH KH	4CST (I)	9H 8C — 6D 5S
j3CSF (Y)	j 9H — — — 5H	2CRF (Jh)	JH TH
j4CFL	j 9H 6H 3H	2CSF (O)	9H 8H
jLP (T)	j TH	2CRF (Qh)	QH JH
jLP (9-5)	j 9H	2CSF (I)	9H — 7H
jLP (J)	j JH	3CFL	9H 5H 2H
j4CST (I)	j 9H 8C — 6D	2CRF (Kh)	KH QH
jLP (Q)	j QH	2CSF (D)	9H — — 6H
jDraw Four	j QH JC 3D 2S	3CST (O)	9H 8C 7D
		1CRF (T)	TH
		1MC (9-5)	9H
		Draw Five	QH 9C 6D 4S 2H

(2P 15-6-4-3)

Symbol Key

j : Joker   O : Open-ended
RF : Royal Flush   I : Inside
SF : Straight Flush   D : Double-Inside
FH : Full House   Y : Triple-Inside
FL : Flush
ST : Straight
2P : Two Pair
LP : Low Pair (Usually A-2, Aces to Twos)
MC : Middle Card

5K,4K,etc. : 5 of a Kind, 4 of a Kind, etc.
4C,3C,etc. : 4-Card, 3-Card, etc.
Ah,Kh,etc. : Ace-high, King-high, etc.

Example

j4CST (D) : Joker 4-Card Straight, Double-Inside

JOKER WILD KINGS OR BETTER TABLES
20-7-5-3 MACHINE

Payoff Table

Final Hand	1 Coin	5 Coins
Royal Flush	400	4700
Five of a Kind	200	(5 X 200)
Joker Royal Flush	100	(5 X 100)
Straight Flush	50	(5 X 50)
Four of a Kind	20	(5 X 20)
Full House	7	(5 X 7)
Flush	5	(5 X 5)
Straight	3	(5 X 3)
Three of a Kind	2	(5 X 2)
Two Pair	1	(5 X 1)
Pair of Kings or Better	1	(5 X 1)

Long-Term Machine Payback

Fixed Royal Flush Payoff	Machine Payback
5000 (5 Coins)	101.1%
4700 (5 Coins)	101.0%
4000 (5 Coins)	100.6%
400 (1 Coin)	99.6%

Minimum Progressive Royal Flush
Jackpot Needed for 100% Machine Payback

$ 142.39 (5 Nickels)
     711.95 (5 Quarters)
   2,847.79 (5 Dollars)

Minimum Progressive Royal Flush
Jackpot Needed for 101% Machine Payback

$ 239.08 (5 Nickels)
   1,195.39 (5 Quarters)
   4,781.56 (5 Dollars)

Short-Term Win/Loss Odds

Odds of Winning	Odds of Losing
39%	61%

Playing Strategy

Joker Hand	Example	Regular Hand	Example
j5K	j 9H 9C 9D 9S	RF	AH KH QH JH TH
jRF	j AH KH QH JH	SF	9H 8H 7H 6H 5H
jSF	j 9H 8H 7H 6H	4CRF	KH QH JH TH
j4K	j 9H 9C 9D	4K	9H 9C 9D 9S
j4CRF	j QH JH TH	FH	9H 9C 8D 8S 8H
jFH	j 9H 9C 8D 8S	FL	9H 7H 5H 3H 2H
j4CSF (O)	j 9H 8H 7H	3K	9H 9C 9D
jFL	j 9H 7H 5H 3H	4CSF	9H 8H 7H 6H
j4CSF (I)	j 9H 8H — 6H	ST	9H 8C 7D 6S 5H
j4CSF (D 1HC)	j 5H 4H — — AH	2P	9H 9C 8D 8S
j3K	j 9H 9C	3CRF	QH JH TH
j4CSF (D 0HC)	j 9H 8H — — 5H	HP	AH AC
jST	j 9H 8C 7D 6S	4CFL	9H 7H 5H 3H
j3CRF (Kh)	j KH QH	3CSF (O)	9H 8H 7H
j4CFL (2HC)	j AH KH 6H	LP	9H 9C
j4CFL (1HC)	j AH 9H 6H	4CST (O Kh)	KH QC JD TS
j3CRF (Jh)	j JH TH	3CSF (I)	9H 8H — 6H
j3CRF (Ah)	j AH KH	3CSF (D 1HC)	KH — — TH 9H
j3CSF (O)	j 9H 8H	2CRF (Ah 2HC)	AH KH
j3CRF (Qh)	j QH JH	4CST (O 0HC)	9H 8C 7D 6S
j3CSF (Y 1HC)	j 5H — — — AH	3CSF (D 0HC)	9H 8H — — 5H
j3CSF (I)	j 9H — 7H	2CRF (Kh)	KH QH
jHP	j AH	2CRF (Ah 1HC)	AH TH
j3CSF (D)	j 9H — — 6H	2HC	AH KC
j4CFL (0HC)	j 9H 6H 3H	1CRF (1HC)	AH
j4CST (O <Qh)	j 9H 8C 7D	2CRF (0HC)	JH TH
jLP (T)	j TH	Draw Five	QH 9C 6D 4S 2H
jLP (9-5)	j 9H		
jDraw Four	j QH JC 3D 2S		

(KB 20-7-5-3)

Symbol Key

j : Joker	O : Open-ended
RF : Royal Flush	I : Inside
SF : Straight Flush	D : Double-Inside
FH : Full House	Y : Triple-Inside
FL : Flush	< : Less Than
ST : Straight	
2P : Two Pair	
HP : High Pair (Aces to Kings)	
LP : Low Pair (Usually Q-2, Queens to Twos)	

5K,4K,etc.   : 5 of a Kind, 4 of a Kind, etc.
4C,3C,etc.   : 4-Card, 3-Card, etc.
Ah,Kh,etc.   : Ace-high, King-high, etc.
1HC,0HC,etc. : 1 High Card (King to Ace), etc.

Example

j4CST (D) : Joker 4-Card Straight, Double-Inside

JOKER WILD KINGS OR BETTER TABLES
17-7-5-3 MACHINE

Payoff Table

Final Hand	1 Coin	5 Coins
Royal Flush	400	4700
Five of a Kind	200	(5 X 200)
Joker Royal Flush	100	(5 X 100)
Straight Flush	50	(5 X 50)
Four of a Kind	17	(5 X 17)
Full House	7	(5 X 7)
Flush	5	(5 X 5)
Straight	3	(5 X 3)
Three of a Kind	2	(5 X 2)
Two Pair	1	(5 X 1)
Pair of Kings or Better	1	(5 X 1)

Long-Term Machine Payback

Fixed Royal Flush Payoff	Machine Payback
5000 (5 Coins)	98.5%
4700 (5 Coins)	98.4%
4000 (5 Coins)	98.0%
400 (1 Coin)	97.0%

Minimum Progressive Royal Flush
Jackpot Needed for 100% Machine Payback

$ 391.07 (5 Nickels)
  1,955.37 (5 Quarters)
  7,821.48 (5 Dollars)

Minimum Progressive Royal Flush
Jackpot Needed for 101% Machine Payback

$ 486.86 (5 Nickels)
  2,434.30 (5 Quarters)
  9,737.20 (5 Dollars)

Short-Term Win/Loss Odds

Odds of Winning	Odds of Losing
35%	65%

Playing Strategy

Joker Hand	Example	Regular Hand	Example
j5K	j 9H 9C 9D 9S	RF	AH KH QH JH TH
jRF	j AH KH QH JH	SF	9H 8H 7H 6H 5H
jSF	j 9H 8H 7H 6H	4CRF	KH QH JH TH
j4K	j 9H 9C 9D	4K	9H 9C 9D 9S
j4CRF	j QH JH TH	FH	9H 9C 8D 8S 8H
jFH	j 9H 9C 8D 8S	FL	9H 7H 5H 3H 2H
j4CSF (O)	j 9H 8H 7H	4CSF	9H 8H 7H 6H
jFL	j 9H 7H 5H 3H	3K	9H 9C 9D
j4CSF (I)	j 9H 8H — 6H	ST	9H 8C 7D 6S 5H
j4CSF (D)	j 9H 8H — — 5H	2P	9H 9C 8D 8S
j3K	j 9H 9C	3CRF	QH JH TH
jST	j 9H 8C 7D 6S	HP	AH AC
j3CRF (Kh)	j KH QH	4CFL	9H 7H 5H 3H
j4CFL (2HC)	j AH KH 6H	3CSF (O)	9H 8H 7H
j4CFL (1HC)	j AH 9H 6H	LP	9H 9C
j3CRF (Jh)	j JH TH	4CST (O Kh)	KH QC JD TS
j3CRF (Ah)	j AH KH	3CSF (I)	9H 8H — 6H
j3CSF (O)	j 9H 8H	3CSF (D 1HC)	KH — — TH 9H
j3CRF (Qh)	j QH JH	2CRF (Ah 2HC)	AH KH
j3CSF (Y 1HC)	j 5H — — — AH	4CST (O 0HC)	9H 8C 7D 6S
j3CSF (I)	j 9H — 7H	3CSF (D 0HC)	9H 8H — — 5H
j4CST (I Kh)	j KH QC — TD	2CRF (Kh)	KH QH
jHP	j AH	2CRF (Ah 1HC)	AH TH
j4CFL (0HC)	j 9H 6H 3H	2HC	AH KC
j3CSF (D)	j 9H — — 6H	1CRF (1HC)	AH
j4CST (O <Qh)	j 9H 8C 7D	2CRF (0HC)	JH TH
jLP (T)	j TH	Draw Five	QH 9C 6D 4S 2H
jLP (9-5)	j 9H		
jDraw Four	j QH JC 3D 2S		

(KB 17-7-5-3)

Symbol Key

j : Joker	O : Open-ended
RF : Royal Flush	I : Inside
SF : Straight Flush	D : Double-Inside
FH : Full House	Y : Triple-Inside
FL : Flush	< : Less Than
ST : Straight	
2P : Two Pair	
HP : High Pair (Aces to Kings)	
LP : Low Pair (Usually Q-2, Queens to Twos)	

5K,4K,etc.   : 5 of a Kind, 4 of a Kind, etc.
4C,3C,etc.   : 4-Card, 3-Card, etc.
Ah,Kh,etc.   : Ace-high, King-high, etc.
1HC,0HC,etc. : 1 High Card (King to Ace), etc.

Example

j4CST (D) : Joker 4-Card Straight, Double-Inside

JOKER WILD KINGS OR BETTER TABLES
15-8-5-3 MACHINE

Payoff Table

Final Hand	1 Coin	5 Coins
Royal Flush	400	4000
Five of a Kind	200	(5 X 200)
Joker Royal Flush	100	(5 X 100)
Straight Flush	50	(5 X 50)
Four of a Kind	15	(5 X 15)
Full House	8	(5 X 8)
Flush	5	(5 X 5)
Straight	3	(5 X 3)
Three of a Kind	2	(5 X 2)
Two Pair	1	(5 X 1)
Pair of Kings or Better	1	(5 X 1)

Long-Term Machine Payback

Fixed Royal Flush Payoff	Machine Payback
5000 (5 Coins)	98.4%
4700 (5 Coins)	98.2%
4000 (5 Coins)	97.9%
400 (1 Coin)	96.9%

Minimum Progressive Royal Flush
Jackpot Needed for 100% Machine Payback

$ 414.18	(5 Nickels)
2,070.89	(5 Quarters)
8,283.57	(5 Dollars)

Minimum Progressive Royal Flush
Jackpot Needed for 101% Machine Payback

$ 514.90	(5 Nickels)
2,574.50	(5 Quarters)
10,298.00	(5 Dollars)

Short-Term Win/Loss Odds

Odds of Winning	Odds of Losing
34%	66%

Playing Strategy

Joker Hand	Example	Regular Hand	Example
j5K	j 9H 9C 9D 9S	RF	AH KH QH JH TH
jRF	j AH KH QH JH	SF	9H 8H 7H 6H 5H
jSF	j 9H 8H 7H 6H	4CRF	KH QH JH TH
j4K	j 9H 9C 9D	4K	9H 9C 9D 9S
jFH	j 9H 9C 8D 8S	FH	9H 9C 8D 8S 8H
j4CRF	j QH JH TH	FL	9H 7H 5H 3H 2H
j4CSF (O)	j 9H 8H 7H	4CSF	9H 8H 7H 6H
jFL	j 9H 7H 5H 3H	3K	9H 9C 9D
j4CSF (I)	j 9H 8H — 6H	ST	9H 8C 7D 6S 5H
j4CSF (D)	j 9H 8H — — 5H	2P	9H 9C 8D 8S
j3K	j 9H 9C	3CRF (Qh)	QH JH TH
jST	j 9H 8C 7D 6S	3CRF (Kh)	KH QH JH
j3CRF (Kh)	j KH QH	3CRF (Ah 2HC)	AH KH TH
j4CFL (2HC)	j AH KH 6H	HP	AH AC
j4CFL (1HC)	j AH 9H 6H	3CRF (Ah 1HC)	AH JH TH
j3CRF (Jh)	j JH TH	4CFL	9H 7H 5H 3H
j3CRF (Ah)	j AH KH	3CSF (O)	9H 8H 7H
j3CSF (O)	j 9H 8H	LP	9H 9C
j3CRF (Qh)	j QH JH	4CST (O Kh)	KH QC JD TS
j3CSF (Y 1HC)	j 5H — — — AH	3CSF (I)	9H 8H — 6H
j3CSF (I)	j 9H — 7H	3CSF (D 1HC)	KH — — TH 9H
j4CST (I Kh)	j KH QC — TD	2CRF (Ah 2HC)	AH KH
jHP	j AH	4CST (O 0HC)	9H 8C 7D 6S
j4CFL (0HC)	j 9H 6H 3H	3CSF (D 0HC)	9H 8H — — 5H
j3CSF (D)	j 9H — — 6H	2CRF (Kh)	KH QH
j4CST (O ‹Qh)	j 9H 8C 7D	2CRF (Ah 1HC)	AH TH
jLP (T)	j TH	2HC	AH KC
jLP (9-5)	j 9H	1CRF (1HC)	AH
jDraw Four	j QH JC 3D 2S	2CRF (0HC)	JH TH
		Draw Five	QH 9C 6D 4S 2H

(KB 15-8-5-3)

Symbol Key

j : Joker		O : Open-ended
RF : Royal Flush		I : Inside
SF : Straight Flush		D : Double-Inside
FH : Full House		Y : Triple-Inside
FL : Flush		‹ : Less Than
ST : Straight			
2P : Two Pair			
HP : High Pair (Aces to Kings)			
LP : Low Pair (Usually Q-2, Queens to Twos)			

5K,4K,etc.   : 5 of a Kind, 4 of a Kind, etc.
4C,3C,etc.   : 4-Card, 3-Card, etc.
Ah,Kh,etc.   : Ace-high, King-high, etc.
1HC,0HC,etc. : 1 High Card (King to Ace), etc.

Example

j4CST (D) : Joker 4-Card Straight, Double-Inside

JOKER WILD KINGS OR BETTER TABLES
15-7-5-3 MACHINE

Payoff Table

Final Hand	1 Coin	5 Coins
Royal Flush	300, 400	4700
Five of a Kind	200	(5 X 200)
Joker Royal Flush	100	(5 X 100)
Straight Flush	50	(5 X 50)
Four of a Kind	15	(5 X 15)
Full House	7	(5 X 7)
Flush	5	(5 X 5)
Straight	3	(5 X 3)
Three of a Kind	2	(5 X 2)
Two Pair	1	(5 X 1)
Pair of Kings or Better	1	(5 X 1)

Long-Term Machine Payback

Fixed Royal Flush Payoff	Machine Payback
5000 (5 Coins)	96.8%
4700 (5 Coins)	96.7%
4000 (5 Coins)	96.3%
400 (1 Coin)	95.3%
300 (1 Coin)	95.0%

Minimum Progressive Royal Flush
Jackpot Needed for 100% Machine Payback

$ 553.81 (5 Nickels)
    2,769.07 (5 Quarters)
   11,076.29 (5 Dollars)

Minimum Progressive Royal Flush
Jackpot Needed for 101% Machine Payback

$ 649.60 (5 Nickels)
    3,248.00 (5 Quarters)
   12,992.01 (5 Dollars)

Short-Term Win/Loss Odds

Odds of Winning	Odds of Losing
31%	69%

Playing Strategy

Joker Hand	Example	Regular Hand	Example
j5K	j 9H 9C 9D 9S	RF	AH KH QH JH TH
jRF	j AH KH QH JH	SF	9H 8H 7H 6H 5H
jSF	j 9H 8H 7H 6H	4CRF	KH QH JH TH
j4K	j 9H 9C 9D	4K	9H 9C 9D 9S
j4CRF	j QH JH TH	FH	9H 9C 8D 8S 8H
jFH	j 9H 9C 8D 8S	FL	9H 7H 5H 3H 2H
j4CSF (O)	j 9H 8H 7H	4CSF	9H 8H 7H 6H
jFL	j 9H 7H 5H 3H	3K	9H 9C 9D
j4CSF (I)	j 9H 8H — 6H	ST	9H 8C 7D 6S 5H
j4CSF (D)	j 9H 8H — — 5H	2P	9H 9C 8D 8S
j3K	j 9H 9C	3CRF	QH JH TH
jST	j 9H 8C 7D 6S	HP	AH AC
j3CRF (Kh)	j KH QH	4CFL	9H 7H 5H 3H
j4CFL (2HC)	j AH KH 6H	3CSF (O)	9H 8H 7H
j4CFL (1HC)	j AH 9H 6H	LP	9H 9C
j3CRF (Jh)	j JH TH	4CST (O Kh)	KH QC JD TS
j3CRF (Ah)	j AH KH	3CSF (I)	9H 8H — 6H
j3CSF (O)	j 9H 8H	3CSF (D 1HC)	KH — — TH 9H
j3CRF (Qh)	j QH JH	2CRF (Ah 2HC)	AH KH
j3CSF (Y 1HC)	j 5H — — — AH	4CST (O 0HC)	9H 8C 7D 6S
j3CSF (I)	j 9H — 7H	3CSF (D 0HC)	9H 8H — — 5H
j4CST (I Kh)	j KH QC — TD	2CRF (Kh)	KH QH
jHP	j AH	2CRF (Ah 1HC)	AH TH
j4CFL (0HC)	j 9H 6H 3H	2HC	AH KC
j3CSF (D)	j 9H — — 6H	1CRF (1HC)	AH
j4CST (O <Qh)	j 9H 8C 7D	2CRF (0HC)	JH TH
jLP (T)	j TH	Draw Five	QH 9C 6D 4S 2H
jLP (9-5)	j 9H		
jDraw Four	j QH JC 3D 2S		

(KB 15-7-5-3)

Symbol Key

j : Joker	O : Open-ended
RF : Royal Flush	I : Inside
SF : Straight Flush	D : Double-Inside
FH : Full House	Y : Triple-Inside
FL : Flush	< : Less Than
ST : Straight	
2P : Two Pair	
HP : High Pair (Aces to Kings)	
LP : Low Pair (Usually Q-2, Queens to Twos)	

5K,4K,etc. : 5 of a Kind, 4 of a Kind, etc.
4C,3C,etc. : 4-Card, 3-Card, etc.
Ah,Kh,etc. : Ace-high, King-high, etc.
1HC,0HC,etc. : 1 High Card (King to Ace), etc.

Example

j4CST (D) : Joker 4-Card Straight, Double-Inside

JOKER WILD KINGS OR BETTER TABLES
20-5-4-3 MACHINE

Payoff Table

Final Hand	1 Coin	5 Coins
Royal Flush	500	4000
Five of a Kind	200	(5 X 200)
Joker Royal Flush	100	(5 X 100)
Straight Flush	40	(5 X 40)
Four of a Kind	20	(5 X 20)
Full House	5	(5 X 5)
Flush	4	(5 X 4)
Straight	3	(5 X 3)
Three of a Kind	2	(5 X 2)
Two Pair	1	(5 X 1)
Pair of Kings or Better	1	(5 X 1)

Long-Term Machine Payback

Fixed Royal Flush Payoff	Machine Payback
5000 (5 Coins)	95.9%
4700 (5 Coins)	95.7%
4000 (5 Coins)	95.4%
500 (1 Coin)	94.7%

Minimum Progressive Royal Flush
Jackpot Needed for 100% Machine Payback

$ 677.33 (5 Nickels)
    3,386.09 (5 Quarters)
   13,544.36 (5 Dollars)

Minimum Progressive Royal Flush
Jackpot Needed for 101% Machine Payback

$ 780.83 (5 Nickels)
    3,904.15 (5 Quarters)
   15,616.62 (5 Dollars)

Short-Term Win/Loss Odds

Odds of Winning	Odds of Losing
32%	68%

Playing Strategy

Joker Hand	Example	Regular Hand	Example
j5K	j 9H 9C 9D 9S	RF	AH KH QH JH TH
jRF	j AH KH QH JH	SF	9H 8H 7H 6H 5H
jSF	j 9H 8H 7H 6H	4K	9H 9C 9D 9S
j4K	j 9H 9C 9D	4CRF	KH QH JH TH
j4CRF	j QH JH TH	FH	9H 9C 8D 8S 8H
j4CSF (O)	j 9H 8H 7H	FL	9H 7H 5H 3H 2H
jFH	j 9H 9C 8D 8S	3K	9H 9C 9D
j4CSF (I)	j 9H 8H — 6H	4CSF (O)	9H 8H 7H 6H
jFL	j 9H 7H 5H 3H	ST	9H 8C 7D 6S 5H
j3K	j 9H 9C	4CSF (I)	9H 8H — 6H 5H
j4CSF (D)	j 9H 8H — — 5H	3CRF (Kh)	KH QH JH
jST	j 9H 8C 7D 6S	2P	9H 9C 8D 8S
j3CRF (Kh)	j KH QH	3CRF (Qh)	QH JH TH
j3CRF (Ah)	j AH KH	3CRF (Ah 2HC)	AH KH TH
j3CRF (Jh)	j JH TH	HP	AH AC
j4CFL (2HC)	j AH KH 6H	3CRF (Ah 1HC)	AH JH TH
j4CFL (1HC)	j AH 9H 6H	4CFL	9H 7H 5H 3H
j3CSF (O)	j 9H 8H	LP	9H 9C
j3CRF (Qh)	j QH JH	3CSF (O)	9H 8H 7H
j3CSF (Y 1HC)	j 5H — — — AH	4CST (O)	9H 8C 7D 6S
j4CST (I Kh)	j KH QC — TD	2CRF (Ah 2HC)	AH KH
jHP	j AH	3CSF (I)	9H 8H — 6H
j3CSF (I)	j 9H — 7H	3CSF (D 1HC)	KH — — TH 9H
j4CST (O <Jh)	j 9H 8C 7D	2CRF (Kh)	KH QH
j3CSF (D)	j 9H — — 6H	2HC	AH KC
j4CST (O Jh)	j JH TC 9D	2CRF (Ah 1HC)	AH TH
jLP (T)	j TH	1CRF (1HC)	AH
jLP (9-5)	j 9H	3CSF (D 0HC)	9H 8H — — 5H
jDraw Four	j QH JC 3D 2S	2CRF (0HC)	JH TH
		Draw Five	QH 9C 6D 4S 2H

(KB 20-5-4-3)

Symbol Key

j	: Joker	O	: Open-ended
RF	: Royal Flush	I	: Inside
SF	: Straight Flush	D	: Double-Inside
FH	: Full House	Y	: Triple-Inside
FL	: Flush	<	: Less Than
ST	: Straight		
2P	: Two Pair		
HP	: High Pair (Aces to Kings)		
LP	: Low Pair (Usually Q-2, Queens to Twos)		

5K,4K,etc.   : 5 of a Kind, 4 of a Kind, etc.
4C,3C,etc.   : 4-Card, 3-Card, etc.
Ah,Kh,etc.   : Ace-high, King-high, etc.
1HC,0HC,etc. : 1 High Card (King to Ace), etc.

Example

j4CST (D) : Joker 4-Card Straight, Double-Inside

JOKER WILD JACKS OR BETTER TABLES
10-5-4-3 MACHINE

Payoff Table

Final Hand	1 Coin	5 Coins
Royal Flush	500	4700
Five of a Kind	250	(5 X 250)
Joker Royal Flush	200	(5 X 200)
Straight Flush	50	(5 X 50)
Four of a Kind	10	(5 X 10)
Full House	5	(5 X 5)
Flush	4	(5 X 4)
Straight	3	(5 X 3)
Three of a Kind	2	(5 X 2)
Two Pair	1	(5 X 1)
Pair of Jacks or Better	1	(5 X 1)

Long-Term Machine Payback

Fixed Royal Flush Payoff	Machine Payback
5000 (5 Coins)	98.6%
4700 (5 Coins)	98.4%
4000 (5 Coins)	98.0%
500 (1 Coin)	97.2%

Minimum Progressive Royal Flush
Jackpot Needed for 100% Machine Payback

$ 378.51 (5 Nickels)
  1,892.56 (5 Quarters)
  7,570.25 (5 Dollars)

Minimum Progressive Royal Flush
Jackpot Needed for 101% Machine Payback

$ 467.48 (5 Nickels)
  2,337.39 (5 Quarters)
  9,349.57 (5 Dollars)

Short-Term Win/Loss Odds

Odds of Winning	Odds of Losing
25%	75%

Playing Strategy

Joker Hand	Example	Regular Hand	Example
j5K	j 9H 9C 9D 9S	RF	AH KH QH JH TH
jRF	j AH KH QH JH	SF	9H 8H 7H 6H 5H
jSF	j 9H 8H 7H 6H	4CRF	KH QH JH TH
j4K	j 9H 9C 9D	4K	9H 9C 9D 9S
j4CRF	j QH JH TH	FH	9H 9C 8D 8S 8H
j4CSF (O)	j 9H 8H 7H	4CSF (O)	9H 8H 7H 6H
j4CSF (I)	j 9H 8H — 6H	FL	9H 7H 5H 3H 2H
jFH	j 9H 9C 8D 8S	3K	9H 9C 9D
jFL	j 9H 7H 5H 3H	ST	9H 8C 7D 6S 5H
j4CSF (D)	j 9H 8H — — 5H	4CSF (I)	9H 8H — 6H 5H
j3K	j 9H 9C	3CRF	QH JH TH
jST	j 9H 8C 7D 6S	2P	9H 9C 8D 8S
j3CRF	j JH TH	HP	AH AC
j3CSF (I 1HC)	j JH — 9H	4CFL	9H 7H 5H 3H
j3CSF (O)	j 9H 8H	4CST (O 3HC)	KH QC JD TS
j4CST (O *HC)	j QH JC TD	3CSF (O)	9H 8H 7H
j3CSF (D 1HC)	j QH — — 9H	3CSF (I *HC)	QH JH — 9H
j4CFL (1HC)	j AH 9H 6H	4CST (O 2HC)	QH JC TD 9S
j3CSF (I 0HC)	j 9H — 7H	2CRF (Qh 2HC)	QH JH
j3CSF (Y 1HC)	j 5H — — — AH	2CRF (Kh 2HC)	KH QH
j4CST (I *HC)	j QH JC — 9D	4CST (O 1HC)	JH TC 9D 8S
j3CSF (D 0HC)	j 9H — — 6H	LP	9H 9C
jHP (J)	j JH	2CRF (Ah 2HC)	AH KH
jHP (Q)	j QH	3CSF (I 0HC)	9H 8H — 6H
j4CST (O <Th)	j 9H 8C 7D	4CST (O 0HC)	9H 8C 7D 6S
jHP (K)	j KH	3CSF (D 1HC)	KH — — TH 9H
jHP (A)	j AH	2CRF (1HC)	AH TH
j4CST (O Th)	j TH 9C 8D	1CRF (J)	JH
jLP (T)	j TH	1CRF (Q)	QH
jLP (9-5)	j 9H	1CRF (K)	KH
jDraw Four	j QH JC 3D 2S	1CRF (A)	AH
		3CSF (D 0HC)	9H 8H — — 5H
		Draw Five	QH 9C 6D 4S 2H

(JB 10-5-4-3)

Symbol Key

```
        j : Joker              O : Open-ended
       RF : Royal Flush        I : Inside
       SF : Straight Flush     D : Double-Inside
       FH : Full House         Y : Triple-Inside
       FL : Flush              < : Less Than
       ST : Straight           * : One or More
       2P : Two Pair
       HP : High Pair (Aces to Jacks)
       LP : Low Pair (Usually T-2, Tens to Twos)


       5K,4K,etc.    : 5 of a Kind, 4 of a Kind, etc.
       4C,3C,etc.    : 4-Card, 3-Card, etc.
       Ah,Kh,etc.    : Ace-high, King-high, etc.
       1HC,0HC,etc.  : 1 High Card (Ace to Jack), etc.
```

Example

```
       j4CST (O *HC) : Joker 4-Card Straight, Open-
                       ended, One or More High Cards
```

JOKER WILD JACKS OR BETTER TABLES
6-4-3-3 MACHINE

Payoff Table

Final Hand	1 Coin	5 Coins
Royal Flush	500	4000
Five of a Kind	250	(5 X 250)
Joker Royal Flush	200	(5 X 200)
Straight Flush	50	(5 X 50)
Four of a Kind	6	(5 X 6)
Full House	4	(5 X 4)
Flush	3	(5 X 3)
Straight	3	(5 X 3)
Three of a Kind	2	(5 X 2)
Two Pair	1	(5 X 1)
Pair of Jacks or Better	1	(5 X 1)

Long-Term Machine Payback

Fixed Royal Flush Payoff	Machine Payback
5000 (5 Coins)	92.1%
4700 (5 Coins)	92.0%
4000 (5 Coins)	91.6%
500 (1 Coin)	90.7%

Minimum Progressive Royal Flush
Jackpot Needed for 100% Machine Payback

$ 948.97 (5 Nickels)
  4,744.85 (5 Quarters)
 18,979.38 (5 Dollars)

Minimum Progressive Royal Flush
Jackpot Needed for 101% Machine Payback

$ 1,037.96 (5 Nickels)
   5,189.81 (5 Quarters)
  20,759.23 (5 Dollars)

Short-Term Win/Loss Odds

Odds of Winning	Odds of Losing
12%	88%

Playing Strategy

Joker Hand	Example	Regular Hand	Example
j5K	j 9H 9C 9D 9S	RF	AH KH QH JH TH
jRF	j AH KH QH JH	SF	9H 8H 7H 6H 5H
jSF	j 9H 8H 7H 6H	4CRF	KH QH JH TH
j4CRF	j QH JH TH	4K	9H 9C 9D 9S
j4K	j 9H 9C 9D	FH	9H 9C 8D 8S 8H
j4CSF	j 9H 8H 7H	4CSF (O)	9H 8H 7H 6H
jFH	j 9H 9C 8D 8S	FL	9H 7H 5H 3H 2H
jFL	j 9H 7H 5H 3H	ST	9H 8C 7D 6S 5H
j3K	j 9H 9C	4CSF (I)	9H 8H — 6H 5H
jST	j 9H 8C 7D 6S	3K	9H 9C 9D
j3CRF	j JH TH	3CRF	QH JH TH
j3CSF (I 1HC)	j JH — 9H	2P	9H 9C 8D 8S
j3CSF (O)	j 9H 8H	HP	AH AC
j4CST (O *HC)	j QH JC TD	3CSF (O)	9H 8H 7H
j3CSF (D 1HC)	j QH — — 9H	4CFL	9H 7H 5H 3H
j3CSF (I 0HC)	j 9H — 7H	3CSF (I *HC)	QH JH — 9H
j4CST (I *HC)	j QH JC — 9D	4CST (O *HC)	QH JC TD 9S
j3CSF (Y 1HC)	j 5H — — — AH	2CRF (Qh 2HC)	QH JH
j4CST (O <Th)	j 9H 8C 7D	2CRF (Kh 2HC)	KH QH
j4CFL (1HC)	j AH 9H 6H	LP	9H 9C
jHP (J)	j JH	2CRF (Ah 2HC)	AH KH
j3CSF (D 0HC)	j 9H — — 6H	4CST (O 0HC)	9H 8C 7D 6S
jHP (Q)	j QH	4CST (I 3HC)	KH QC JD 9S
jHP (A)	j AH	3CSF (I 0HC)	9H 8H — 6H
j4CST (O Th)	j TH 9C 8D	3CSF (D 1HC)	KH — — TH 9H
jHP (K)	j KH	2CRF (1HC)	AH TH
jLP (T)	j TH	1CRF (J)	JH
jLP (9-5)	j 9H	1CRF (Q)	QH
jDraw Four	j QH JC 3D 2S	1CRF (K)	KH
		1CRF (A)	AH
		3CSF (D 0HC)	9H 8H — — 5H
		Draw Five	QH 9C 6D 4S 2H

(JB 6-4-3-3)

Symbol Key

j :	Joker	O : Open-ended
RF :	Royal Flush	I : Inside
SF :	Straight Flush	D : Double-Inside
FH :	Full House	Y : Triple-Inside
FL :	Flush	< : Less Than
ST :	Straight	* : One or More
2P :	Two Pair	
HP :	High Pair (Aces to Jacks)	
LP :	Low Pair (Usually T-2, Tens to Twos)	

```
5K,4K,etc.   : 5 of a Kind, 4 of a Kind, etc.
4C,3C,etc.   : 4-Card, 3-Card, etc.
Ah,Kh,etc.   : Ace-high, King-high, etc.
1HC,0HC,etc. : 1 High Card (Ace to Jack), etc.
```

Example

j4CST (O *HC) : Joker 4-Card Straight, Open-
                ended, One or More High Cards

JOKER WILD ACES OR BETTER TABLES
20-6-5-3 MACHINE

Payoff Table

Final Hand	1 Coin	5 Coins
Royal Flush	500	4000
Five of a Kind	200	(5 X 200)
Joker Royal Flush	100	(5 X 100)
Straight Flush	50	(5 X 50)
Four of a Kind	20	(5 X 20)
Full House	6	(5 X 6)
Flush	5	(5 X 5)
Straight	3	(5 X 3)
Three of a Kind	2	(5 X 2)
Two Pair	1	(5 X 1)
Pair of Aces or Better	1	(5 X 1)

Long-Term Machine Payback

Fixed Royal Flush Payoff	Machine Payback
5000 (5 Coins)	94.3%
4700 (5 Coins)	94.1%
4000 (5 Coins)	93.8%
500 (1 Coin)	93.1%

Minimum Progressive Royal Flush
Jackpot Needed for 100% Machine Payback

$ 842.51 (5 Nickels)
  4,212.55 (5 Quarters)
 16,850.19 (5 Dollars)

Minimum Progressive Royal Flush
Jackpot Needed for 101% Machine Payback

$ 945.91 (5 Nickels)
  4,729.56 (5 Quarters)
 18,918.24 (5 Dollars)

Short-Term Win/Loss Odds

Odds of Winning	Odds of Losing
30%	70%

Playing Strategy

Joker Hand	Example	Regular Hand	Example
j5K	j 9H 9C 9D 9S	RF	AH KH QH JH TH
jRF	j AH KH QH JH	SF	9H 8H 7H 6H 5H
jSF	j 9H 8H 7H 6H	4K	9H 9C 9D 9S
j4K	j 9H 9C 9D	4CRF	KH QH JH TH
j4CRF	j QH JH TH	FH	9H 9C 8D 8S 8H
jFH	j 9H 9C 8D 8S	FL	9H 7H 5H 3H 2H
j4CSF (O)	j 9H 8H 7H	4CSF	9H 8H 7H 6H
jFL	j 9H 7H 5H 3H	3K	9H 9C 9D
j4CSF (I)	j 9H 8H — 6H	ST	9H 8C 7D 6S 5H
j3K	j 9H 9C	2P	9H 9C 8D 8S
j4CSF (D)	j 9H 8H — — 5H	3CRF (Qh)	QH JH TH
jST	j 9H 8C 7D 6S	HP	AH AC
j4CFL (1HC)	j AH 9H 6H	3CRF (Kh)	KH QH JH
j3CRF (Ah)	j AH KH	3CRF (Ah)	AH KH QH
j3CRF (Jh)	j JH TH	4CFL	9H 7H 5H 3H
j3CSF (Y 1HC)	j 5H — — — AH	3CSF (O)	9H 8H 7H
j3CSF (O)	j 9H 8H	LP	9H 9C
j3CRF (Qh)	j QH JH	3CSF (I)	9H 8H — 6H
jHP	j AH	3CSF (D 1HC)	KH — — TH 9H
j3CSF (I)	j 9H — 7H	4CST (O)	9H 8C 7D 6S
j3CRF (Kh)	j KH QH	3CSF (D 0HC)	9H 8H — — 5H
j4CFL (0HC)	j 9H 6H 3H	2CRF (Ah)	AH KH
j3CSF (D)	j 9H — — 6H	1CRF (1HC)	AH
j4CST (O)	j 9H 8C 7D	2CRF (Jh)	JH TH
jLP (T)	j TH	2CRF (Qh)	QH JH
j3CSF (Y 0HC)	j 9H — — — 5H	4CST (I)	9H 8C — 6D 5S
jLP (J)	j JH	3CFL	9H 5H 2H
jLP (9-5)	j 9H	2CRF (Kh)	KH QH
jDraw Four	j QH JC 3D 2S	2CSF (O)	9H 8H
		2CSF (I)	9H — 7H
		Draw Five	QH 9C 6D 4S 2H

(AB 20-6-5-3)

Symbol Key

j	: Joker	O	: Open-ended
RF	: Royal Flush	I	: Inside
SF	: Straight Flush	D	: Double-Inside
FH	: Full House	Y	: Triple-Inside
FL	: Flush	<	: Less Than
ST	: Straight		
2P	: Two Pair		
HP	: High Pair (Aces)		
LP	: Low Pair (Usually K-2, Kings to Twos)		

5K,4K,etc.   : 5 of a Kind, 4 of a Kind, etc.
4C,3C,etc.   : 4-Card, 3-Card, etc.
Ah,Kh,etc.   : Ace-high, King-high, etc.
1HC,0HC,etc. : 1 High Card (Ace), etc.

Example

        j4CST (D) : Joker 4-Card Straight, Double-Inside

Joker Wild Two Pair or Better
20-8-7-5 Machine

Final Hand	1 Coin Payoff	
RF	500	1)
5K	100	
SF	50	2)
4K	20	
FH	8	
FL	7	
ST	5	
3K	2	
2P	1	

Notes:

1) 5 Coin Payoff = 5000.

2) Joker Royal Flush counts as Straight Flush.

(See back side for strategy.)

Joker Wild Two Pair or Better
20-10-6-5 Machine

Final Hand	1 Coin Payoff	
RF	500	1)
5K	100	
SF	50	2)
4K	20	
FH	10	
FL	6	
ST	5	
3K	2	
2P	1	

Notes:

1) 5 Coin Payoff = 5000.

2) Joker Royal Flush counts as Straight Flush.

(See back side for strategy.)

Joker Wild Two Pair or Better
20-8-7-6 Machine

Final Hand	1 Coin Payoff	
RF	500	1)
5K	100	
SF	50	2)
4K	20	
FH	8	
FL	7	
ST	6	
3K	2	
2P	1	

Notes:

1) 5 Coin Payoff = 5000.

2) Joker Royal Flush counts as Straight Flush.

(See back side for strategy.)

2P 20-8-7-6 Playing Strategy

Joker Hand	Regular Hand
J5K	RF
JRF	SF
JSF	4CRF
J4K	4K
JFH	FH
JFL	FL
J4CRF (Qh)	ST
J4CSF (O)	4CSF
JST	4CSF
J4CSF	3K
J4CRF (Kh)	3CRF (Qh)
J4CRF (I)	ST
J4CRF (Ah)	3CRF (Kh)
J4CSF (D)	3CRF (Jh)
J3K	4CFL
J3CSF (O)	LP
J3CSF (D)	4CST (I)
J3CRF (Jh)	3CSF (D)
J3CSF (I)	3CSF (I)
J4CFL	2CRF (Ah)
J3CRF (Qh)	3CSF (O)
J3CSF (Y)	3CST (O)
J3CSF (I)	3CSF (Y)
J3CRF (Kh)	2CRF (Kh)
J3CRF (Ah)	2CRF (I)
J3CST (O)	2CSF (D)
J3CSF (D)	2CRF (Ah)
J3CST (I)	2CSF (I)
J3CST (T)	3CST (I)
J3CSF (Y)	2CSF (Y)
JLP (9-5)	2CST (O)
JLP (J)	
JLP (Q)	Draw Five

2P 20-10-6-5 Playing Strategy

Joker Hand	Regular Hand
J5K	RF
JRF	SF
JSF	4CRF
J4K	4K
JFH	FH
JFL	FL
J4CRF (Qh)	ST
J4CSF (O)	4CSF
J4K	3K
J3K	4CSF
J4CSF (O)	LP
J4CRF (Jh)	3CSF (O)
J3CRF (Jh)	4CFL
J4CST (I)	4CST (I)
J4CFL	LP
J3CSF (Ah)	3CSF (O)
J3CSF (O)	3CFL
J3CSF (D)	2CRF (Qh)
J3CRF (Kh)	2CRF (Kh)
J3CSF (O)	3CST (O)
J3CST (O)	3CSF (D)
J2CRF (Qh)	4CST (I)
J4CST (I)	2CRF (Ah)
J3CFL	3CSF (I)
J3CSF (D)	2CSF (D)
J2CRF (Kh)	2CRF (I)
J2CRF (I)	2CSF (O)
JLP (T)	2CSF (I)
JLP (9-5)	1CRF (T)
JLP (J)	2CSF (D)
JLP (Q)	2CSF (I)
J4CST (D)	2CSF (Y)
	Draw Five

2P 20-8-7-5 Playing Strategy

Joker Hand	Regular Hand
J5K	RF
JRF	SF
JSF	4CRF
J4K	4K
JFH	FH
JFL	FL
J4CRF (Qh)	ST
J4CSF (O)	4CSF
JST	3K
JFL	4CSF
J4CRF (Kh)	2P
J4CRF (I)	3CRF (Qh)
J4CRF (Ah)	3K
J4CSF (D)	3CRF (Kh)
J3K	3CFL
J4CSF (O)	LP
J3CRF (Jh)	3CSF (D)
J3CSF (O)	4CST (I)
J3CSF (I)	3CSF (I)
J4CFL	2CRF (Qh)
J3CRF (Qh)	3CRF (Jh)
J3CSF (Y)	2CRF (Kh)
J3CSF (I)	2CRF (O)
J3CRF (Kh)	3CSF (O)
J3CRF (Ah)	3CST (O)
J3CST (O)	3CSF (Y)
J3CSF (D)	2CRF (I)
J3CST (I)	2CSF (D)
J3CST (T)	2CSF (Y)
JLP (J)	1CRF (T)
JLP (9-5)	3CST (I)
JLP (Q)	Draw Five
J4CST (D)	

Joker Wild Two Pair or Better
25-8-5-4 Machine

Final Hand	1 Coin Payoff	
RF	500	1)
5K	100	
SF	50	2)
4K	25	
FH	8	
FL	5	
ST	4	
3K	2	
2P	1	

Notes:

1) 5 Coin Payoff = 5000.

2) Joker Royal Flush counts as Straight Flush.

(See back side for strategy.)

Joker Wild Two Pair or Better
20-8-6-5 Machine

Final Hand	1 Coin Payoff	
RF	500	1)
5K	100	
SF	50	2)
4K	20	
FH	8	
FL	6	
ST	5	
3K	2	
2P	1	

Notes:

1) 5 Coin Payoff = 5000.

2) Joker Royal Flush counts as Straight Flush.

(See back side for strategy.)

Joker Wild Two Pair or Better
16-8-5-4 Machine

Final Hand	1 Coin Payoff	
5K	400	1)
SF	100	2)
4K	16	
FH	8	
FL	5	
ST	4	
3K	2	
2P	1	

Notes:

1) 5 Coin Payoff = 4000.

2) Regular and Joker Royal Flushes count as Straight Flushes.

(See back side for strategy.)

2P 16-8-5-4
Playing Strategy

Joker Hand	Regular Hand
5K	RF
RF	SF
SF	4K
4K	FH
FH	4CSF (O)
4CRF (Qh)	4CSF (Ah)
4CSF (O)	4CSF (I)
4CSF (Kh)	FL
4CSF (I)	3K
FL	ST
FH	2P
4CRF (Ah)	3CRF (Qh)
4CRF (D)	4CFL
FL	4CST (O)
3K	3CSF (Kh)
ST	3CSF (I)
2P	4CST (O)
3CSF (Jh)	3CSF (D)
3CSF (O)	4CST (I)
3CRF (Qh)	3CRF (Ah)
3CSF (I)	2CRF (Qh)
4CST (O)	2CRF (Ah)
3CSF (Kh)	1CRF (D)
3CRF (Ah)	2CSF (D)
3CSF (D)	2CRF (Kh)
3CSF (Y)	2CSF (Y)
3CRF (Ah)	1MC (9-5)
4CST (I)	Draw Five
3CRF (I)	
LP (T)	
LP (9-5)	
LP (J)	
3CST (O)	
LP (Q)	
Draw Four	

2P 20-8-6-5
Playing Strategy

Joker Hand	Regular Hand
5K	RF
RF	SF
SF	4CRF
4K	4CRF
FH	4K
4CRF (Qh)	FH
4CSF (O)	FL
4CSF (Kh)	ST
4CSF (Ah)	4CSF
FL	3K
FH	4CSF
ST	2P
4CRF (I)	3K
4CRF (Kh)	3CRF
3K	4CFL
4CSF (D)	4CST (O)
4CRF (Ah)	4CSF (D)
3CSF (O)	3CSF (I)
3CRF (Jh)	3CSF (Qh)
3CSF (O)	4CST (I)
3CRF (Qh)	3CSF (D)
3CSF (I)	3CRF (I)
4CST (O)	LP
3CSF (Kh)	2CRF (Qh)
3CSF (D)	2CRF (Ah)
4CST (I)	1CRF (D)
4CFL	2CSF (I)
3CRF (Ah)	2CSF (D)
3CSF (Y)	1CRF (T)
3CRF (Ah)	2CRF (Kh)
3CST (O)	2CSF (I)
LP (T)	3CST (I)
LP (9-5)	2CSF (Y)
LP (J)	Draw Five
4CST (D)	
LP (Q)	

2P 25-8-5-4
Playing Strategy

Joker Hand	Regular Hand
5K	RF
RF	SF
SF	4K
4K	4CRF
FH	FH
4CRF (Qh)	FL
4CSF (O)	ST
4CSF (Kh)	4CSF (I)
4CSF (I)	4CSF (Kh)
4CRF (Qh)	3K
FL	ST
FH	2P
4CRF (Ah)	3CRF
4CSF (D)	4CFL
4CRF (Kh)	LP
4CST (I)	3CSF (O)
4CFL	3CRF (Qh)
3CRF (Kh)	2CRF (Qh)
3CSF (D)	2CSF (O)
3CRF (Qh)	2CRF (Jh)
3CSF (Qh)	4CST (I)
4CST (O)	3CSF (D)
3CSF (I)	3CSF (I)
3CRF (Ah)	4CST (O)
3CSF (Y)	2CSF (I)
LP (T)	2CRF (Ah)
LP (9-5)	3CST (O)
LP (J)	2CSF (D)
3CST (O)	3CFL
LP (Q)	2CRF (Kh)
Draw Four	1CRF (T)
	Draw Five

Joker Wild Two Pair or Better
20-8-5-4 Machine

Final Hand	1 Coin Payoff	
RF	500	1)
5K	100	
SF	50	2)
4K	20	
FH	8	
FL	5	
ST	4	
3K	2	
2P	1	

Notes:

1) 5 Coin Payoff = 5000
   or
   10 Coin Payoff = 10,000.

2) Joker Royal Flush counts as Straight Flush.

(See back side for strategy.)

Joker Wild Two Pair or Better
15-6-5-4 Machine

Final Hand	1 Coin Payoff	
5K	400	1)
SF	100	2)
4K	15	
FH	6	
FL	5	
ST	4	
3K	2	
2P	1	

Notes:

1) 5 Coin Payoff = 4000.

2) Regular and Joker Royal Flushes count as Straight Flushes.

(See back side for strategy.)

Joker Wild Two Pair or Better
20-8-6-4 Machine

Final Hand	1 Coin Payoff	
RF	500	1)
5K	100	
SF	50	2)
4K	20	
FH	8	
FL	6	
ST	4	
3K	2	
2P	1	

Notes:

1) 5 Coin Payoff = 5000.

2) Joker Royal Flush counts as Straight Flush.

(See back side for strategy.)

2P 20-8-6-4
Playing Strategy

Joker Hand	Regular Hand
5K	RF
RF	SF
SF	4CRF
4K	4K
FH	FH
FL	FL
4CRF (Qh)	4CSF (O)
4CSF (O)	4CRF (Kh)
4CRF (Kh)	4CSF (I)
FL	3K
ST	ST
4CRF (Kh)	4CSF (I)
4CSF (I)	3CRF
4CRF (Ah)	4CFL
2P	3CSF (O)
ST	4CSF (O)
4CSF (D)	LP
3K	3CSF (I)
3CRF (Qh)	3CSF (D)
4CSF (O)	4CST (O)
3CSF (O)	3CRF (Qh)
LP	3CSF (Kh)
4CSF (I)	4CST (I)
3CSF (D)	3CRF (Jh)
4CFL	3CRF (Ah)
3CSF (I)	3CSF (D)
3CRF (Qh)	2CRF (Qh)
3CSF (Kh)	4CST (I)
3CRF (Kh)	3CSF (O)
3CRF (D)	2CRF (I)
3CSF (D)	2CRF (Qh)
3CSF (I)	2CRF (Ah)
2CRF (Jh)	2CRF (Kh)
2CSF (Y)	3CSF (D)
3CSF (Y)	4CST (I)
3CRF (Ah)	3CST (O)
4CST (I)	2CSF (D)
2CRF (Kh)	2CSF (I)
2CRF (Qh)	LCRF (T)
2CRF (Ah)	2CSF (Y)
LP (T)	
2CSF (D)	
3CST (O)	
2CSF (O)	
LP (J)	
LCRF (T)	
LP (9-5)	
2CSF (Y)	
LP (Q)	
Draw Four	Draw Five

2P 15-6-5-4
Playing Strategy

Joker Hand	Regular Hand
5K	RF
RF	SF
SF	4K
4K	FH
FH	4CSF (O)
FL	4CRF (Kh)
4CRF (Qh)	4CRF (Ah)
4CSF (O)	4CSF (I)
4CRF (Kh)	FL
4CSF (I)	3K
FH	ST
FL	FL
4CRF (Ah)	ST
4CSF (D)	2P
3K	3CRF (Qh)
ST	4CSF (O)
FL	4CFL
2P	LP
3CSF (Qh)	3CRF (Kh)
3CSF (O)	3CSF (I)
3CRF (Qh)	4CST (O)
3CSF (O)	LP
3CSF (I)	3CSF (I)
4CST (I)	4CST (O)
3CRF (Qh)	3CRF (Ah)
4CSF (O)	3CSF (D)
3CSF (D)	4CST (I)
3CRF (Kh)	3CSF (O)
3CSF (D)	2CRF (Qh)
4CFL	4CST (I)
3CSF (Ah)	3CRF (Jh)
4CST (I)	2CRF (Qh)
2CRF (Jh)	2CSF (I)
2CSF (Y)	2CRF (Ah)
3CSF (Y)	3CST (O)
LP (T)	2CRF (D)
LP (9-5)	2CRF (Kh)
LP (J)	2CSF (D)
3CST (O)	2CSF (Y)
LP (Q)	2CRF (Ah)
Draw Four	2CSF (Y)
	1MC (9-5)
	LCRF (T)
	Draw Five

2P 20-8-5-4
Playing Strategy

Joker Hand	Regular Hand
5K	RF
RF	SF
SF	4K
4K	4CRF
FH	FH
FL	FL
4CRF (Qh)	4CSF (O)
4CSF (O)	4CRF (Kh)
4CRF (Kh)	4CRF (Ah)
FL	4CSF (I)
ST	3K
4CRF (Kh)	ST
4CSF (I)	2P
4CRF (Ah)	3CRF
4CFL	4CFL
4CRF (Ah)	3CSF (O)
4CSF (D)	4CSF (O)
3CSF (I)	LP
4CSF (O)	3CSF (I)
4CST (O)	3CSF (D)
3CSF (I)	4CST (I)
3CRF (Qh)	3CRF (Jh)
4CST (I)	4CST (I)
3CSF (I)	2CRF (Qh)
4CFL	2CRF (Jh)
3CRF (Ah)	2CRF (Ah)
3CSF (Kh)	2CRF (Kh)
2CRF (Jh)	3CFL
2CRF (Qh)	3CSF (I)
2CSF (Y)	2CRF (I)
LP (T)	2CRF (Ah)
3CST (O)	3CST (O)
LP (9-5)	2CSF (D)
LP (J)	2CSF (O)
LP (Q)	LCRF (T)
Draw Four	Draw Five

Joker Wild Two Pair or Better
15-6-4-3 Machine

Final Hand	1 Coin Payoff
5K	500 1)
SF	100 2)
4K	15
FH	6
FL	4
ST	3
3K	2
2P	1

Notes:

1) 5 Coin Payoff = 4000
   or
   10 Coin Payoff = 8000.

2) Regular and Joker Royal Flushes count as Straight Flushes.

(See back side for strategy.)

Joker Wild Two Pair or Better
20-10-4-3 Machine

Final Hand	1 Coin Payoff
RF	500 1)
5K	100
SF	50 2)
4K	20
FH	10
FL	4
ST	3
3K	2
2P	1

Notes:

1) 5 Coin Payoff = 5000.

2) Joker Royal Flush counts as Straight Flush.

(See back side for strategy.)

(Unused Card)

2P 20-10-4-3 Playing Strategy

Joker Hand	Regular Hand
5K	RF
RF	SF
SF	4CRF
4K	4K
FH	FH
4CRF (Qh)	3K
4CSF (O)	FL
4CRF (Kh)	4CSF (O)
4CSF (I)	ST
3K	4CSF (I)
FL	2P
4CSF (Ah)	3CRF
4CRF (D)	4CFL
ST	LP
3CSF (Jh)	4CSF (O)
3CRF (O)	4CST (O)
3CSF (Qh)	3CSF (I)
3CSF (I)	3CSF (D)
4CST (O)	3CSF (Jh)
3CRF (Kh)	4CST (I)
3CSF (D)	2CRF (Qh)
4CFL	2CRF (Kh)
3CSF (Ah)	2CRF (Ah)
3CRF (T)	2CSF (O)
3CSF (Y)	2CSF (I)
2CRF (Ah)	2CRF (Ah)
LP (T)	3CFL
LP (9-5)	2CSF (D)
LP (J)	1CRF (T)
4CST (I)	Draw Five
LP (Q)	
3CST (O)	
Draw Four	

2P 15-6-4-3 Playing Strategy

Joker Hand	Regular Hand
5K	RF
RF	SF
SF	4K
4K	FH
FH	4CRF (Kh)
4CRF (Qh)	4CSF (O)
4CSF (O)	4CRF (Ah)
4CRF (Kh)	4CSF (I)
4CRF (Ah)	3K
4CSF (I)	FL
FH	ST
3K	2P
FL	3CRF (Qh)
ST	3CSF (O)
3CSF (Qh)	3CRF (Kh)
3CRF (Jh)	3CSF (I)
4CST (O)	LP
3CSF (O)	4CST (O)
3CRF (Kh)	3CRF (Ah)
3CSF (I)	3CSF (D)
3CRF (Kh)	4CST (I)
3CSF (D)	2CRF (Qh)
4CST (O)	2CRF (Kh)
4CST (I)	2CRF (Qh)
3CSF (Ah)	2CSF (O)
3CRF (Ah)	2CSF (I)
3CSF (Y)	3CFL
4CFL	2CRF (Kh)
LP (T)	2CSF (D)
LP (9-5)	2CSF (O)
LP (J)	1CRF (T)
4CST (I)	1MC (9-5)
LP (Q)	Draw Five
Draw Four	

Joker Wild Kings or Better
15-8-5-3 Machine

Final Hand	1 Coin Payoff
RF	400 1)
5K	200
JRF	100
SF	50
4K	15
FH	8
FL	5
ST	3
3K	2
2P	1
KB	1

Notes:

1) 5 Coin Payoff = 4000.

(See back side for strategy.)

Joker Wild Kings or Better
17-7-5-3 Machine

Final Hand	1 Coin Payoff
RF	400 1)
5K	200
JRF	100
SF	50
4K	17
FH	7
FL	5
ST	3
3K	2
2P	1
KB	1

Notes:

1) 5 Coin Payoff = 4700.

(See back side for strategy.)

Joker Wild Kings or Better
20-7-5-3 Machine

Final Hand	1 Coin Payoff
RF	400 1)
5K	200
JRF	100
SF	50
4K	20
FH	7
FL	5
ST	3
3K	2
2P	1
KB	1

Notes:

1) 5 Coin Payoff = 4700.

(See back side for strategy.)

KB 20-7-5-3

Playing Strategy

Joker Hand	Regular Hand
5K	RF
RF	SF
SF	4CRF
4K	4K
4CRF	FH
FH	FL
4CSF (O)	3K
FL	4CSF
4CSF (I)	ST
4CSF (D 1HC)	2P
3K	3CRF
4CSF (D OHC)	4CFL
ST	HP
3CRF (Kh)	4CFL
4CFL (2HC)	3CSF (O)
4CFL (1HC)	LP
3CRF (Jh)	4CFL (2HC)
3CRF (Ah)	4CFL (1HC)
3CSF (O)	4CST (O Kh)
3CRF (Qh)	3CSF (I)
3CSF (Y 1HC)	3CSF (D I)
3CSF (I)	2CRF (Ah 2HC)
HP	4CST (O OHC)
3CSF (D)	3CSF (D OHC)
4CFL (OHC)	2CRF (Kh)
4CST (O <Qh)	2CRF (Ah 1HC)
LP (T)	2HC
LP (9-5)	1CRF (1HC)
Draw Four	2CRF (OHC)
	Draw Five

KB 17-7-5-3

Playing Strategy

Joker Hand	Regular Hand
5K	RF
RF	SF
SF	4CRF
4K	4K
4CRF	FH
FH	FL
4CSF (O)	4CSF
FL	3K
4CSF (I)	ST
4CSF (D)	2P
3K	3CRF
4CSF (D)	HP
ST	4CFL
3CRF (Kh)	3CSF (O)
4CFL (2HC)	LP
4CFL (1HC)	4CST (O Kh)
3CRF (Jh)	3CSF (I)
3CRF (Ah)	3CSF (D I)
3CRF (Qh)	2CRF (Ah 2HC)
3CSF (O)	4CST (O OHC)
3CSF (Y 1HC)	3CSF (D OHC)
3CSF (I)	2CRF (Kh)
HP	2CRF (Ah 1HC)
3CSF (D)	2HC
4CFL (OHC)	1CRF (1HC)
4CST (O <Qh)	2CRF (OHC)
LP (T)	Draw Five
LP (9-5)	
Draw Four	

KB 15-8-5-3

Playing Strategy

Joker Hand	Regular Hand
5K	RF
RF	SF
SF	4CRF
4K	4K
4CRF	FH
FH	FL
4CSF (O)	3CRF (Qh)
FL	3CRF (Ah 2HC)
4CSF (I)	3CRF (Kh)
4CSF (D)	HP
3K	3CRF (Ah 1HC)
4CSF (D)	4CFL
ST	3CSF (O)
3CRF (Kh)	LP
4CFL (2HC)	4CST (O Kh)
4CFL (1HC)	3CSF (I)
3CRF (Jh)	3CSF (D I)
3CRF (Ah)	4CST (O OHC)
3CRF (Qh)	3CSF (D OHC)
3CSF (O)	2CRF (Ah 2HC)
LP	3CSF (D Kh)
3CSF (Y 1HC)	2CRF (Kh)
3CSF (I)	2CRF (Ah 1HC)
HP	2HC
3CSF (D)	1CRF (1HC)
4CFL (OHC)	2CRF (OHC)
4CST (O <Qh)	Draw Five
LP (T)	
LP (9-5)	
Draw Four	

Joker Wild Kings or Better
20-5-4-3 Machine

Final Hand	1 Coin Payoff
RF	500 1)
5K	200
JRF	100
SF	40
4K	20
FH	5
FL	4
ST	3
3K	2
2P	1
KB	1

Notes:

1) 5 Coin Payoff = 4000
   or
   10 Coin Payoff = 8000.

(See back side for strategy.)

(Unused Card)

KB 20-5-4-3
Playing Strategy

Joker Hand	Regular Hand
5K	RF
RF	SF
SF	4K
4K	4CRF
4CRF	FH
FH	FL
4CSF (O)	3K
FL	ST
3K	4CSF (I)
4CSF (D)	4CSF (Kh)
4CSF (I)	3CRF (Qh)
ST	2P
4CSF (Kh)	3CRF (Ah 2HC)
3CRF (Ah)	HP
3CRF (Qh)	3CRF (Ah 1HC)
4CFL (2HC)	4CFL
3CRF (Jh)	LP
4CFL (1HC)	3CSF (O)
3CSF (O)	4CST (O)
3CRF (Y 1HC)	3CRF (Ah 2HC)
4CST (I Kh)	3CSF (I)
HP	3CSF (D 1HC)
3CSF (I)	2HC
4CST (O <Jh)	3CRF (Ah 1HC)
3CSF (D)	1CRF (1HC)
4CST (O Jh)	3CSF (D OHC)
LP (T)	3CRF (OHC)
LP (9-5)	Draw Five
Draw Four	

Joker Wild Aces or Better
20-6-5-3 Machine

Final Hand	1 Coin Payoff	
RF	500	1)
5K	200	
JRF	100	
SF	50	
4K	20	
FH	6	
FL	5	
ST	3	
3K	2	
2P	1	
AB	1	

Notes:

1) 5 Coin Payoff = 4000.

(See back side for strategy.)

Joker Wild Jacks or Better
6-4-3-3 Machine

Final Hand	1 Coin Payoff	
RF	500	1)
5K	250	
JRF	200	
SF	50	
4K	6	
FH	4	
FL	3	
ST	3	
3K	2	
2P	1	
JB	1	

Notes:

1) 5 Coin Payoff = 4000.

(See back side for strategy.)

Joker Wild Jacks or Better
10-5-4-3 Machine

Final Hand	1 Coin Payoff	
RF	500	1)
5K	250	
JRF	200	
SF	50	
4K	10	
FH	5	
FL	4	
ST	3	
3K	2	
2P	1	
JB	1	

Notes:

1) 5 Coin Payoff = 4700.

(See back side for strategy.)

JB 10-5-4-3
Playing Strategy

Joker Hand	Regular Hand
5K	RF
RF	SF
SF	4CRF
4K	4K
4CRF	FH
4CSF (O)	FL
4CSF (I)	3K
FH	ST
FL	4CSF (D)
3K	4CSF (I)
4CSF (D)	3CRF
ST	2P
3CRF	HP
3CSF (I 1HC)	4CFL
3CSF (I 1HC)	3CSF (O 3HC)
4CST (O *HC)	4CST (O)
3CSF (D 1HC)	3CSF (I *HC)
4CFL (1HC)	4CST (O 2HC)
3CSF (I OHC)	2CRF (Qh 2HC)
3CSF (Y 1HC)	2CRF (Kh 2HC)
4CST (I *HC)	4CST (O 1HC)
4CST (D OHC)	LP
HP (J)	2CRF (Ah 2HC)
HP (Q)	3CSF (I OHC)
4CST (O <Th)	4CST (O OHC)
HP (K)	3CSF (O)
HP (A)	3CSF (D 1HC)
4CST (O Th)	2CRF (J)
LP (T)	1CRF (Q)
LP (9-5)	1CRF (K)
Draw Four	1CRF (A)
	2CRF (1HC)
	3CSF (D OHC)
	Draw Five

JB 6-4-3-3
Playing Strategy

Joker Hand	Regular Hand
5K	RF
RF	SF
SF	4CRF
4K	4K
4CRF	FH
4CSF	FL
4K	ST
FH	4CSF (O)
FL	3K
3K	4CSF (I)
ST	2P
3CSF (I)	3CRF
3CSF (O)	HP
4CST (O *HC)	3CSF (O)
3CSF (D 1HC)	4CFL
3CSF (I OHC)	4CST (O)
4CST (I OHC)	3CSF (I *HC)
3CSF (I *HC)	3CSF (I OHC)
4CST (Y 1HC)	4CST (I 3HC)
4CST (O <Th)	4CST (O OHC)
4CFL (1HC)	2CRF (Qh 2HC)
HP (J)	2CRF (Kh 2HC)
HP (Q)	LP
HP (A)	2CRF (Ah 2HC)
4CST (O Th)	3CSF (I OHC)
HP (K)	3CSF (D 1HC)
4CST (O Th)	2CRF (J)
LP (K)	1CRF (Q)
LP (T)	1CRF (K)
LP (9-5)	1CRF (A)
Draw Four	2CRF (1HC)
	3CSF (D OHC)
	Draw Five

AB 20-6-5-3
Playing Strategy

Joker Hand	Regular Hand
5K	RF
RF	SF
SF	4K
4K	4CRF
4CRF	FH
FH	FL
FL	4CSF
4CSF	3K
3K	4CSF
4CSF (O)	ST
4CSF (I)	2P
4CSF (D)	3CRF (Qh)
2P	HP
ST	3CRF (Ah)
3CRF (Qh)	4CFL
HP	3CRF (Kh)
4CFL (1HC)	3CRF (Ah)
3CRF (Kh)	1CRF (1HC)
3CRF (Ah)	1CRF (Jh)
4CFL	2CRF (Qh)
3CSF (D OHC)	2CRF (Kh)
3CSF (I)	4CST (O)
4CST (O)	3CSF (O)
3CSF (O)	LP
3CSF (Y 1HC)	3CSF (I)
HP	3CSF (D 1HC)
3CSF (I)	4CST (I)
3CSF (D 1HC)	3CRF
LP	2CRF (Kh)
3CSF (Y OHC)	2CSF (O)
LP (J)	2CRF (Ah)
LP (T)	2CSF (I)
LP (9-5)	Draw Five
Draw Four	